Anointing with the Spirit
The Rite
of Confirmation
The Use of Oil and Chrism

Studies in the Reformed Rites
of the Catholic Church,
Volume II

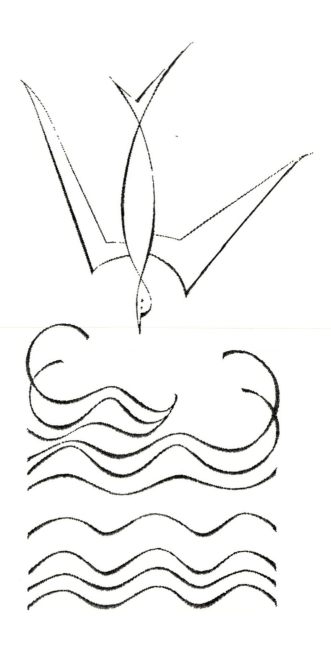

Gerard Austin, O.P.

Anointing with the Spirit

The Rite of Confirmation: The Use of Oil and Chrism

A PUEBLO BOOK

Liturgical Press Collegeville, Minnesota

Design by Frank Kacmarcik, Obl.S.B.

A Pueblo Book published by Liturgical Press.

ISBN: 0-8146-6070-3

For those responsible for the
Institute for Ecumenical and Cultural Research
Collegeville, Minnesota
where ecumenical dialogue takes place
in an atmosphere of scholarship and charity
for the good of the church.

Contents

Introduction

For several years now I have been teaching a graduate course on the sacraments of initiation. On the very first day of class I ask my students to write down the answers to the following questions: (1) Is the Holy Spirit given at baptism? If so, what is the difference between that bestowal and the gift of the Spirit at confirmation? (2) At what age should the sacrament of confirmation normally be conferred, and why? (3) Should the practice of infant baptism be retained, and why? I am always amazed at the variety of answers that is turned in.

It is with this practical awareness of the variety of current opinions concerning confirmation that I begin this work. I realize that such a variety of opinions is not a new phenomenon. No other sacrament has had such a checkered history. No other sacrament has changed so frequently in ritual, prayers, and meaning through the centuries. Alexander Schmemann writes: "No other liturgical act of the Church has provoked more theological controversies than this second sacrament of initiation; none has received a greater variety of interpretations."[1]

The Second Vatican Council was prudent enough to refrain from offering anything definitive on the nature of confirmation but spoke in broad terms that attempted to keep everyone happy: "By the sacrament of Confirmation they [the baptized] are more perfectly bound to the Church and are endowed with the special strength of the Holy Spirit. Hence they are, as true witnesses of Christ, more strictly obliged to spread the faith by word and deed."[2] By far the most important statement the Council made about confirmation was that it should be viewed in the larger context of the initiation process: "The rite of confirmation is also to be revised in order that the intimate connection of this sacrament with the whole of Christian initiation may stand out more clearly."[3] Confirmation's connection with the total initiation process is the touchstone for an understanding of the sacrament. It was stressed by Paul VI in the opening words of his Apostolic Constitution, *Divinae Consortium Naturae*, which promulgated the new rite of confirmation:

"The sharing in the divine nature which is granted to men through the grace of Christ has a certain likeness to the origin, development, and nourishing of natural life. The faithful are born anew by baptism, strengthened by the sacrament of confirmation, and finally are sustained by the food of eternal life in the eucharist. By means of these sacraments of Christian initiation, they thus receive in increasing measure the treasures of divine life and advance toward the perfection of charity."[4]

More and more in the church today it is realized that initiation is a complex, ongoing process and not simply a series of isolated ritual moments. This larger, more comprehensive view of initiation might be called "baptismal consciousness." I believe this baptismal consciousness is beginning to mark the piety of our day. In this vein, my book presupposes the views on baptism put forth in the first volume of the present series, *Studies in the Reformed Rites of the Catholic Church*. If you have not yet read it, I would urge you to put down my book and first read *The Shape of Baptism: The Rite of Christian Initiation.*[5]

The rites that I analyze are *Rite of Confirmation* and *Rite of the Blessing of Oils; Rite of Consecrating the Chrism.* Both were published in 1971.[6] These analyses will in turn provide deeper insights into the rite of *Dedication of a Church and an Altar.*[7]

In choosing the title of my study, *Anointing with the Spirit,* I deliberately use the preposition "with." In Acts 10 we read the account of Peter's preaching the word in the house of Cornelius: "The word which was proclaimed throughout all Judea, beginning from Galilee after the baptism which John preached: how God anointed Jesus of Nazareth with the Holy Spirit and with power; how he went about doing good and healing all that were oppressed by the devil, for God was with him" (vss. 37–38). Jesus was anointed with the Spirit, and so are his followers. In the newly composed consecratory prayer of chrism the church prays: "Through the sign of holy chrism, you dispense your life and love to men and women. By anointing them with the Spirit, you strengthen all who have been reborn in baptism. Through that anointing you transform them into the likeness of Christ your Son and give them a share in his royal, priestly, and prophetic work."[8] This emphasis on the anointing with the Spirit into the likeness of Christ reflects a long tradition articulated as early as the second century by St. Irenaeus: "The Father is the one who anoints, the Son is the anointed one, and the Spirit is the chrism."[9]

Part One, "The Tradition," surveys the historical development of confirmation. Part Two, "The Reforms," deals with the modern liturgical reforms: first in the Roman Catholic communion and then in other communions. The chapter treating the reform of the rites of blessing of oils and consecrating chrism includes its own historical background material. Part Three, "The Future," analyzes the present liturgical praxis, with an opening to the future.

I would like to thank Professor Thomas O'Meara of the University of Notre Dame for his generous, ongoing assistance in the task of helping me put my thoughts into written form; Professor Daniel Stevick of the Episcopal Divinity School and Professor Louis Weil of Nashotah House for their help with my treatment of confirmation in the Anglican tradition; and Professor Gabriele Winkler of St. John's University, Collegeville, for her valuable insights, especially those pertaining to the Christian East. Finally, my thanks are extended to Professor Aidan Kavanagh of Yale University for inviting me to be part of Pueblo Publishing Company's series, *Studies in the Reformed Rites of the Catholic Church.* This series, based on the collection *The Rites of the Catholic Church,* has been a great help to many, including myself, and I am proud to be part of it.

Gerard Austin, O.P.

NOTES

1. Alexander Schmemann, *Of Water and the Spirit* (St. Vladimir's Seminary Press, Crestwood, N.Y. 1974), p. 76.

2. *Lumen Gentium* 11. Austin Flannery (ed.), *Vatican Council II: The Conciliar and Post Conciliar Documents* (Liturgical Press, Collegeville, Minn. 1975), p. 361.

3. *Sacrosanctum Concilium* 71. Documents on the Liturgy 1963–1979 (Liturgical Press, Collegeville, Minn. 1982), no. 71.

4. *The Rites of the Catholic Church* (Pueblo, New York 1976), p. 290.

5. Aidan Kavanagh, *The Shape of Baptism: The Rite of Christian Initiation* (Pueblo, New York 1978).

6. *Ordo Confirmationis* (Typis Polyglottis Vaticanis, Vatican City 1971). See *The Rites,* pp. 287–334. *Ordo Benedicendi Oleum Catechumenorum et Infirmorum et Conficiendi Chrisma*

(Typis Polyglottis Vaticanis, Vatican City 1971). See *The Rites,* pp. 515–527.

7. *Ordo Dedicationis Ecclesiae et Altaris* (Typis Polyglottis Vaticanis, Vatican City 1977). See *The Rites of the Catholic Church,* vol. 2 (Pueblo, New York 1980), pp. 185–293.

8. *The Rites,* p. 526.

9. Irenaeus of Lyon, *Adversus Haereses* III, 18, 3 (translation mine). See A. Rousseau and L. Doutreleau (eds.), *Contre Les Hérésies,* Sources Chrétiennes 211 (Cerf, Paris 1974), p. 353.

The Tradition

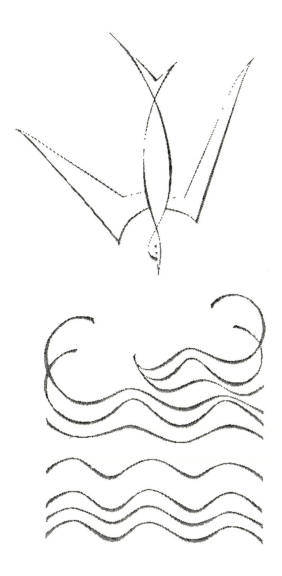

Chapter One

Historical Development of Confirmation

Christian initiation in the New Testament focuses on
two persons: Jesus the Christ and John the Baptizer.
John's baptism was the culmination of a long process of
Old Testament ritual washings. This centuries-long process began with the washing of clothing, objects, and
the like. It evolved into a washing of oneself. Finally
these human bathings were superseded by a bath in
which God took the initiative. The prophet Ezekiel
describes a cleansing to be given not by oneself but
by God:

"For I will take you from the nations, and gather you
from all the countries, and bring you into your own
land. I will sprinkle clean water upon you, and you
shall be clean from all your uncleannesses, and from all
your idols I will cleanse you. . . . I will put my spirit
within you, and cause you to walk in my statutes and
be careful to observe my ordinances" (Ez 36:24–25,27).

As with his preaching, John's baptism pointed beyond
itself. He did not fix attention on himself since his
whole *raison d'être* was to prepare the way for Christ.
His message was eschatological: "Repent, for the kingdom of heaven is at hand" (Mt 3:2). The kingdom is
coming, conversion is called for. This point was grasped
by the early church, as the gospel of Matthew shows:
"For this is he who was spoken of by the prophet
Isaiah when he said, 'The voice of one crying in the

wilderness: Prepare the way of the Lord, make his paths straight' "(Mt 3:3).

BAPTISM OF JESUS BY JOHN

The close connection between Jesus and John is obvious. Both began to preach in the same way: "Repent, for the kingdom of heaven is at hand" (Mt 3:2; 4:17). Both preached ideas that were often not those of contemporary Judaism. But a chief expression of their similarity is that Jesus accepted baptism at the hands of John. That this event really took place seems certain. Such a paradox would hardly have been fabricated by the early church. As John says, "I need to be baptized by you, and do you come to me?" (Mt 3:14).

Jesus' baptism is important. It serves as a revelation of the mystery of salvation in Jesus. Moreover, through the centuries it has become the theological interpretation *par excellence* of Christian initiation. "And when Jesus was baptized, he went up immediately from the water, and behold, the heavens were opened and he saw the Spirit of God descending like a dove, and alighting on him; and lo, a voice from heaven, saying, 'This is my beloved Son, with whom I am well pleased' " (Mt 3:16–17). Jesus is baptized, not for his own sins, but for the sins of others. He is baptized in view of his death, which will cause the Spirit of forgiveness to be given to the church.[1] Thus, after the death of Jesus, his followers continue to use the water-rite as the chief vehicle of expressing the forgiveness of sins and the imparting of the Holy Spirit. Two elements of the Jordan event mark the understanding of Christian baptism down through the centuries: (1) possession by the Spirit; and (2) consciousness of the sonship of God.[2] Just as Jesus was anointed with the Spirit, so his followers will be given the same Spirit. Just as Jesus was declared to be the "beloved Son," so his followers will be declared to be the sons and daughters of God.

4

The Jordan event sets the tone of what Christian initiation is all about.

One could well wonder why the water-rite continued. John the Baptizer had made clear the difference between his baptism and that of Jesus: "I baptize you with water for repentance, but he who is coming after me is mightier than I, whose sandals I am not worthy to carry; he will baptize you with the Holy Spirit and with fire" (Mt 3:11). Does not this statement establish an antithesis between water and Spirit? Jesus himself told his apostles during a postresurrection appearance, "John baptized with water, but before many days you shall be baptized with the Holy Spirit" (Acts 1:5).

The answer to this dilemma lies in the early church's view of initiation essentially as a Spirit event. Aidan Kavanagh writes: "It must be remembered that the baptism of Christians was not johannine but christic: it was a baptism not of water but of Holy Spirit. The water bath is a function of the Spirit. This means that pneumatic data concerning Christian baptism subordinate water data: the latter are to be understood in terms of the former."[3] Has not the Western church forgotten this over the centuries?

In his dialogue with Nicodemus, Jesus says, "Truly, truly, I say to you, unless one is born of water and the Spirit, he cannot enter the kingdom of God" (Jn 3:5). In the Christian tradition, this verse is one of the most important New Testament texts concerning baptism. Yet there have been tremendous differences of opinion concerning the relationship that exists between "water" and "the Spirit." I. de la Potterie writes: "There has been a rather strong tendency in the history of exegesis to subordinate the second term (*pneumatos*) to the first (*hydatos*), that is, to refer all the activity of the Spirit to that which he exerts in the sacrament of baptism. The text of the evangelist does not support this interpretation."[4] This unfortunate subordination of Spirit to water had disastrous results: it boxed in the activity of the Spirit, limiting it to certain isolated ritual moments; it impoverished the water-rite, cutting it off from its other ritual components such as anointings, hand-layings, and so on; and ultimately it led to the disintegration of a once-unified rite of initiation.

It could be argued that the entire complex history of the relationship between baptism and confirmation reduces itself to the varying views of this relationship between "water" and "the Spirit." James Dunn categorizes the trends:

"We have noticed that there are three or four elements and three parties involved in Christian conversion-initiation. Each of these elements and parties could be said to be the characteristic emphasis of each of the three main streams of Christianity. Catholics emphasize the role of the Church and of water-baptism (and laying on of hands); Protestants emphasize the role of the individual and of preaching and faith; Pentecostals emphasize the role of Jesus Christ as Baptizer in the Spirit and of Spirit-baptism."[5]

NEW TESTAMENT EVIDENCE

Keeping in tandem all these elements and parties involved in Christian initiation has proved a difficult task. New Testament evidence does not provide any tidy pattern. Sometimes the Holy Spirit accompanies the water-bath; sometimes the Spirit is given before and thus is proof that nothing "hinders" the baptism.

Especially in the Acts of the Apostles we find a multiplicity of patterns, so many that no one should argue that New Testament evidence sets up this or that pattern as *the* model. In this vein it could be said that the diversity in baptismal practice among the churches today reflects the diversity of New Testament testimony.[6]

The only thing the biblical evidence is certain of is that while the water-bath and the gift of the Spirit are in some way distinguishable, they can never be totally separated. In the Acts baptism appears as the sacrament of faith. Through the operation of the Spirit one is led to conversion by the proclamation of the gospel; the water-bath is the concrete response to apostolic preaching. The whole event is a process, and the whole process is Spirit-filled. That is why certain passages of the Acts are so perplexing. One very difficult text is chapter 8, in which baptism in the name of Jesus is administered by Philip to the Samaritans, but is not accompanied by the gift of the Holy Spirit. After the baptisms Peter and John came down from Jerusalem. "Then they laid their hands on them and they received the Holy Spirit" (Acts 8:17). How could the Samaritans have believed and have been baptized (vs. 12) if the gift of the Spirit had been withheld? Is not the very act of belief a gift of the Spirit?

Scripture scholars have come up with varying solutions to this dilemma. Some think the distinction here between the reception of baptism and the reception of the Spirit is a Lucan device used to insist that the gift of the Spirit comes through the church, represented by the college of the Twelve in Jerusalem.[7] Reginald Fuller writes: "The separation of the laying on of hands [from baptism] in Acts 8 has nothing to do with the western medieval separation of confirmation from baptism but is due rather to Luke's redactional interest in subordinating each successive new stage in the Christian mission to the Jerusalem church and its apostolate."[8]

Conversion, the water-bath, and the gift of the Spirit must never be separated from one another; otherwise all sorts of distortions arise. Furthermore, the third element, the gift of the Spirit, must be seen as the most important of the three elements. The early church did not feel compelled to distinguish between what would later on become known as the two distinct sacraments of baptism and confirmation. Rudolf Schnackenburg writes that "one will seek in vain in the Pauline Letters to discover a peculiar sacrament of the Spirit alongside baptism; the actuality and fulness of the Spirit of God, whose 'outpouring' is most closely connected with baptism, dominates the Apostle's field of vision."[9]

Some authors maintain that two theologies of the Spirit are found in the New Testament: one reflected in the Acts, and one reflected in John and Paul. According to these scholars, for Luke the Spirit in the Acts is the release of a new prophetic force. This force is not related to the forgiveness of sins given in baptism, but follows it, thereby accounting for two separate ritual actions: the water-bath and the imposition of hands, with the latter action being the ritual expression of the giving of the prophetic Spirit. This concept of the Spirit as prophetic Spirit in the Acts would reflect the primitive thinking of the early community. Paul combines this idea with the concept of the life-giving Spirit.[10] This same thinking is reflected in John: "Jesus answered, 'Truly, truly, I say to you, unless one is born of water and the Spirit, he cannot enter the kingdom of God' " (Jn 3:5).

This distinction between life-giving Spirit and prophetic Spirit would be seen by these scholars to provide the basis for the later distinction between baptism and confirmation. Two complementary sacraments would be needed to account for the two complementary aspects of Christology and pneumatology in the one mystery of salvation expressed in the New Testament: life-giving Spirit and prophetic Spirit.

Other scholars argue that the New Testament writings offer no ground for a distinction between baptism and confirmation. Raymond Brown says: "The problem of confirmation as a separate sacrament seems to be a post-New Testament problem."[11]

It would seem that one should look primarily to Paul for a theology of the Spirit, and not to Luke. Luke's view of the Spirit is dominated by the early enthusiastic understanding of the first Christians, whereas among the inspired authors Paul most deserves the title, "the theologian of the Spirit."[12] In Paul's eyes the Spirit is the fundamental mark of belonging to Christ, and the gift of the Spirit is the result of baptism. "For by one Spirit we were all baptized into one body—Jews or Greeks, slaves or free—and all were made to drink of one Spirit" (1 Cor 12:13). For Paul the seal of the Spirit is a gift tied up with baptism and not a postbaptismal gift.[13] The anointing mentioned by Paul in 2 Corinthians 1:21–22 (as in 1 Jn 2:20,27) does not refer to an anointing understood in terms of a rite (later to be called confirmation), but is a spiritual anointing, the anointing of the Christian by faith, which comes about through baptism.[14] For Paul, sacramental dying and rising with Christ is one reality, and it brings about union with the pneuma-Christ. Just as Christ has risen from the dead and is now a pneuma-being, so the baptized follower of Christ attains a "resurrection" that puts him or her in possession of the Spirit.[15] This theological development, as expressed in the Pauline letters, seems far more normative for the theology of the sacraments of initiation than do the disparate practices portrayed in the Acts.

SPHRAGIS

A key for unlocking both the biblical and the patristic understandings of initiation is the concept of *sphragis*, the Greek word that is translated as "seal."[16] It is of particular interest now that the new formula for confirmation contains the Latin word *signaculum*, which came to bear many of the connotations of the word *sphragis*:

"Be sealed with the Gift of the Holy Spirit."[17] The concept of "seal" has a long history in pagan antiquity, in Old Testament and Judaic usages, and in the New Testament and early Christian literature. In the twentieth century it was brought into the limelight by the controversies over confirmation among Anglican scholars. G. W. H. Lampe writes against Dom Gregory Dix and others, who hold that through confirmation one receives the seal of the Spirit by which one is signed for eternity. Lampe maintains: "It is unquestionable that the primary use of the word 'seal,' both among the Fathers and in the Liturgies, relates to Baptism, and not to any of its subsidiary rites."[18] The complexity of the problem arises from the many ways the word was used in patristic tradition. Lampe writes: "The attempt of such writers as Dix and Thorton to find a simple equation between 'sealing' and 'confirmation,' and to proceed to use this equation as a principle by which to interpret the vast number of instances of the term 'seal' in the Fathers, breaks down through their failure to take sufficient account of this bewildering variety of meaning."[19]

The term seal was used not only for what today is considered confirmation, but also for the sign of the cross, for baptism as a whole, and for the water-bath itself. The roots of *sphragis* are both interesting and helpful. There are two principal sources for the concept. One is for the seal with which an owner marked his possessions, as a shepherd would brand his sheep to distinguish them or a Roman general would tattoo the hands or forearms of his soldiers to indicate that they belonged to his regiment. In this sense the early Fathers saw initiation as sealing one as a member of the flock of Christ or of the army of Christ. The second root is derived from the seal used to impress a mark on wax. Such instruments were used especially to seal official documents and wills.

From a very early date in the church's life, certain elements of the baptism complex began to receive varying degrees of attention with varying degrees of emphasis and meaning attached to them. As early as Tertullian we find in his *De Baptismo* (c. 200) the baptismal rite being divided into two parts (the water-bath with its anointing and the imposition of hands) with the gift of the Spirit being attributed to the second part. Tertullian writes: "Not that the Holy Spirit is given to us in the water, but that in the water we are made clean by the action of the angel, and made ready for the Holy Spirit."[20]

Around the year 215 a full description of initiation is offered by Hippolytus in his *Apostolic Tradition.*[21] Over and above the presbyteral postbaptismal anointing a complex action is carried out by the bishop: it contains a hand-laying (not necessarily on each individual candidate), an anointing (an imposition of hand performed with oil), and a signing on the forehead (sealing):

"And the bishop shall lay his hand upon them invoking and saying: 'O Lord God, who didst count these worthy of deserving the forgiveness of sins by the laver of regeneration, make them worthy to be filled with thy Holy Spirit and send upon them thy grace, that they may serve thee according to thy will; to thee is the glory, to the Father and to the Son with the Holy Ghost in the holy Church, both now and ever and world without end. Amen.' After this pouring the consecrated oil and laying his hand on his head, he shall say: 'I anoint thee with holy oil in God the Father Almighty and Christ Jesus and the Holy Ghost.' And sealing him on the forehead, he shall give him the kiss of peace."[22]

To understand the pattern of Hippolytus it must be viewed in its liturgical context, that is, as culminating in the celebration of the eucharist. The pattern of the *Apostolic Tradition* is extremely important because it becomes the "Roman pattern" and will be followed by other Western churches, and then imposed by Rome down through the centuries on the Latin West.[23] The entire history of confirmation in the West is bound up with the periodic insistence by Rome that an indigenous pattern of initiation be replaced by this Roman model.

The completion of the postbaptismal anointing by the presbyter lies in the anointing of the candidate's forehead by the bishop. Pope Innocent I in a letter to Decentius, the bishop of Gubbio, in the year 416 sets the rule quite firmly:

"Concerning the consignation of infants, it is clear that this should not be done by any but the bishop. For presbyters, although they are priests, have not attained the highest rank of the pontificate. The right of bishops alone to seal and to deliver the Spirit the Paraclete is proved not only by the custom of the Church but also by that reading in the Acts of the Apostles which tells how Peter and John were directed to deliver the Holy Spirit to people who were already baptized. For it is permissible for presbyters, either in the absence of a bishop, or when they baptize in his presence, to anoint the baptized with chrism, but only with such as has been consecrated by the bishop: and even then they are not to sign the brow with that oil, for that is reserved to bishops alone when they deliver the Spirit the Paraclete."[24]

This papal insistence on Roman tradition had enormous influence in shaping the development of confirmation in the West by reserving to the bishop the "signing of the brow."

A few years later, in 441, canon two of the First Council of Orange legislates:

12

"None of the ministers who has received the office of
baptizing shall ever proceed without chrism, for we
have agreed that the anointing should be done once;
however, in the case where someone, for whatever
reason, has not been anointed at baptism, let the
bishop be reminded of this in confirmation; as for the
chrism itself, there is in every case but one blessing, not
to prejudice anything, but so that a repeated chrismation not be considered necessary."[25]

The Gallican fathers were speaking of the double chrismation that was going on in rural areas. Gabriele
Winkler provides an interesting examination of the
meaning of this ambiguous canon:

"Quite possibly the situation envisioned by the canon
was the following: on the occasion of his visitation of
rural areas the bishop confirmed, or ratified, the ministry of the local presbyter (or deacon). In the process he
anointed those who had not been anointed when they
were baptized. Perhaps, on the occasion of his visitation he presided at the celebration of the rites of initiation. In that case he anointed those previously baptized
and not anointed along with those whom he was presently baptizing."[26]

Is this "confirmation" a laying on of the hand or an
anointing? Some have interpreted it as a laying on of
the hand, but Winkler argues:

"It may well be that postbaptismal anointing is meant,
and not laying on of the hand. This anointing may or
may not have included a laying on of the hand, but I
do not believe that the rites included a laying on of the
hand *distinct* from the anointing. The laying on of the
hand as a separate rite was customary in Africa (e.g.,
Tertullian, *De baptismo*, viii) and in Rome (e.g., Hippolytus, *Traditio Apostolica*, xxii), but there is no really
clear evidence for the existence of the laying on of the

13

hand as a separate rite in Gaul, except for the reconciliation of heretics."[27]

Her argument is based on the fact that the Gallican missals set out a rite of initiation which is archaic in form, containing only one postbaptismal anointing, done by either the bishop or presbyter at baptism.[28] The First Council of Orange, then, was protecting the unity of the initiation rite.

Another important fifth-century Gallican influence on the history of confirmation was Faustus, who became the abbot of Lerins in 433, and then bishop of Riez in 458. This bishop, who possessed a semi-Pelagian anthropology, delivered a homily on Pentecost that was to play an important role in history.[29] This homily is the first doctrinal explanation of a separated "confirmation ceremony" outside cases of rebaptism and reconciliation of heretics. Dom Gregory Dix goes so far as to call it the base of all medieval theology about confirmation in the West.[30] Faustus states that baptism is complete as to innocence, but as to grace there is a question of its augmentation through confirmation. In baptism we are regenerated to life; after baptism we are confirmed for battle. In baptism we are washed; after baptism we are strengthened.[31] He compares confirmation to the military, because his spirituality and anthropology placed humans in the context of struggle or battle. Confirmation brings the "augmentation in grace," enabling one to take part in the struggle of human life. Confirmation stresses human effort and involvement, whereas baptism is what is passively received. Faustus's words have great influence. They find their way into the *False Decretals*, compiled in the mid-ninth century, and were attributed by Pseudo-Isidore to a certain Pope Melchiades who in fact never existed.[32] This error was passed on in a chain: to Gratian's *Decretum* to Peter Lombard's *Sentences* to Aquinas's *Summa*

Theologiae to scholastic and conciliar teachings, and finally on to popular understanding.

RECONCILIATION OF SCHISMATICS AND HERETICS
Another important factor that influenced initiation liturgy, and confirmation in particular, was the problem of the reconciliation of schismatics and heretics to the true faith. This reconciliation liturgy has a complex history, reflected by the complexity of early church legislation concerning it.

In the East this liturgy of reconciliation gradually expressed itself by the gesture of chrismation more than by the imposition of hands, which was the Western practice. The reason for this is probably to be found in the meaning that chrism took on in disputes over the consubstantiality of the Holy Spirit. In the second century Irenaeus declared that the Father gave the unction, that Christ was the anointed, and the Spirit was the unction.[33] The fourth-century Cappadocian Fathers used this point to show that the Holy Spirit was consubstantial with the Father and the Son. Thus, the role of chrism in the reconciliation liturgies was intimately connected with the very heart of what was being symbolized: the return to orthodox faith.[34]

An interesting question is just how much this reconciliation liturgy affected later Eastern chrismation theology. After the fifth century, postbaptismal anointing was general practice, but previously it had been absent in the East Syrian initiation liturgy, which knew only a prebaptismal anointing. To the question, "What were the factors determining this change in East Syrian practice?" Bernard Botte says:

"It is necessary to take into account a problem which preoccupied the ancient Church, namely, the reception of Christians baptized in heresy into the Church. The position of the Council of Laodicea, as it had been understood at Constantinople in the fifth century was that, if baptism conferred in heresy was valid, the gift of the Spirit was not communicated, and it was necessary to supply it after the baptism. The first time the formula 'Seal of the gift of the Holy Spirit' appears is precisely in this act of reconciliation. From that time on the question could be asked whether this fact did not give rise to the theological reflexion which attempted to show that the gift of the Spirit was separable from baptism and that it was necessary to express this fact by a rite which followed the baptism? Such is the hypothesis that I wish to submit to historians and theologians."[35]

In the West Leo the Great (440–461) used the term "confirmation" in connection with the admission of heretics; those baptized by heretics need only to be confirmed with the invocation of the Holy Spirit through the imposition of hands because they have received the form of baptism without its power.[36] While he probably was not using the term "confirmation" in a technical sense, nevertheless the idea is that reconciliation bestows the Holy Spirit on those entering into the church, since the Spirit cannot work outside the church. Gregory the Great commented that the reconciliation process in the West is accomplished through the imposition of the hand, while in the East it is done through anointing with chrism.[37] All this is not to imply that the postbaptismal rites of initiation and the admission of heretics were the same thing. One could be distinguished from the other, but they followed the same lines of development since they both conferred the Holy Spirit. Some authors would see a "reconfirmation" in the imposition of hands of the reconciliation of heretics.[38] This viewpoint presents a problem, however, since if they were baptized in heresy and schism, apart from the Holy Spirit, they would never have really been confirmed to begin with. As to lines of influence, it would seem that the rite of reconciliation of schismatics and heretics was influenced by the primary example of the bestowal of the Spirit—the postbaptismal rites—and not the other way around, because the very need for reconciliation grew out of the fear that the original initiation in heresy or schism had failed to convey the Holy Spirit.

DISINTEGRATION OF THE RITE OF INITIATION
During the course of the Middle Ages, confirmation gradually became separated not only from the paschal vigil but even from the context of Christian initiation itself. The history of confirmation can be termed a part of the gradual disintegration of the primitive rite of initiation.[39] Since initiatory practices varied greatly during the medieval period in the West, caution must be taken to avoid generalizations; still the overall trend was a movement to separate confirmation from baptism. Impetus to the movement was given by two facts: the existence of large dioceses (especially north of the Alps) making it impossible for frequent visits of the bishop, and the practice of baptizing infants *quamprimum*, as soon as possible after birth.[40] This latter practice was sustained by a growing belief in water baptism as the sole means of salvation. St. Bernard of Clairvaux, for example, wrote in the twelfth century that the way to salvation is closed to unbaptized infants of Christians.[41]

In seventh- and eighth-century Gaul the missals reflect only one postbaptismal anointing. Winkler states, "These liturgical formularies reflect an archaic shape of initiation rites where either the bishop or the presbyter could confer baptism, including the postbaptismal anointing."[42] Leonel Mitchell summarizes the situation: "In sum, none of the Gallican sacramentaries includes a rite of episcopal confirmation, nor have we any evidence requiring us to assume that such a rite was customarily added to the extant baptismal rites, nor that the administration of the single Gallican post-baptismal anointing was confined to bishops."[43] It is only with the Carolingian reform that the role of the bishop according to the Roman pattern was insisted on. The addition of a second anointing by the bishop created a problem in Gallican understanding, and various theologians worked to find a theology for the new practice. The ninth-century archbishop of Mainz, Rabanus Maurus, for example, accounts for what he mistakenly took as two bestowals of the Spirit this way: the presbyteral unction gives the Holy Spirit for a habitation of God; the episcopal unction gives "the grace of the same sevenfold Spirit. . . . with all the fullness of sanctity and of knowledge and of power."[44] This opinion represented a departure from the Roman texts of the Gelasian tradition and that of *Ordo XI*—a "mistaken departure" that has been passed down in history.

Alcuin greatly influenced later thinking by his comment that the imposition of the hand of the bishop confers the Holy Spirit so that the person "may be strengthened through the Holy Spirit to preach to others."[45] Alcuin's "rite" was an attempt to accommodate Roman-papal usage to Gallican needs. In so doing he created a conscious hybridization of the rite. J. D. C. Fisher remarks:

"The most notable feature of Alcuin's rite is the presence of the episcopal hand-laying after the communion of the baptized. Alcuin himself offers no explanation of this unusual sequence, nor does he say how many Churches followed the use which he has outlined in brief. It may be that the Churches which used Alcuin's rite, having been accustomed to an initiation which lacked episcopal hand-laying and anointing, when ordered by Charlemagne to conform to the Roman use, added the missing episcopal acts at the very end rather than break the unity of what had been to them a single and complete entity."[46]

The next blow to the unity of the initiation process was the separation of communion from initiation. Even when newly baptized infants could not be confirmed due to the absence of a bishop, there was no question about their receiving first eucharist after their baptism at the Easter Vigil. What baptism (and ideally confirmation with it) began, eucharist brought to completion. *Ordo Romanus XI,* reflecting the practice of the sixth century, describes baptism and confirmation and then states: "After this they go in to Mass and all the infants receive communion. Care is to be taken lest after they have been baptized they receive any food or suckling before they communicate."[47] Communion would have been the same for infants as for adults (under both species), but after the tenth century (for the sake of convenience, and perhaps as the result of overconcern with infants' spitting up the particles) the practice changed to offering them only the wine. Then, with the disappearance of the laity's communion of the chalice around 1200, infants were left with no communion at all. In 1215, the Fourth Council of the Lateran stated that communion was not obligatory until one reaches the "years of discretion."[48] In the West the final blow was dealt by the Council of Trent, which stated that baptized infants had no need of communion since they were incapable of losing their baptismal grace.[49] There was even an anathema pronounced on those who claimed that infants needed communion before the age of discretion.[50] Such a formulation was unfortunate; it brought about the final dismemberment of the three sacraments of initiation: baptism, confirmation, and eucharist.

In the meantime the notion of confirmation as conferring a particular gift of the Spirit (fortitude) was gaining ground in the popular understanding. The gift that was given was strength for battle (*robur ad pugnam*) and strength to preach to others. This notion followed the thinking of the Gallican writers and opposed the earlier emphasis on the reception of the gift of the Spirit as such and not on the reception of a particular gift. In addition this interpretation was reinforced popularly by the gesture of the confirming bishop being changed from a welcoming kiss of peace into a symbol of spiritual combat—the bishop striking the candidate's cheek.

All this is not to imply that confirmation was a burning issue during this period; it could more rightfully be called the "neglected sacrament." Repeated medieval legislation about its importance confirms the fact that no one was taking it too seriously, neither clergy nor parents. Otherwise such repeated legislation would not have been called for. The moment of conferral of confirmation shows that even its theological connection with the eucharist had been obscured: it was given at the end of the bishop's mass just as other "blessings."[51] In short, confirmation was now standing on its own, totally separated from baptism and at the end of the initiation process.

THE LITURGICAL BOOKS FOR CONFIRMATION
After Hippolytus the earliest full Roman texts of initiation are found in the Gelasian Sacramentary.[52] After the water-bath and the presbyteral anointing on the head with chrism,

"Then the sevenfold Spirit is given to them by the bishop. To seal them (ad consignandum), he lays his hand upon them with these words: 'Almighty God, Father of our Lord Jesus Christ, who has made thy servants to be regenerated of water and the Holy Spirit, and hast given them remission of all their sins, do thou, Lord, send upon them thy Holy Spirit the Paraclete, and give them the spirit of knowledge and godliness, and fill them with the spirit of fear of God, in the name of our Lord Jesus Christ with whom thou livest and reignest ever God with the Holy Spirit, throughout all ages of ages. Amen.' Then he signs them on the forehead with chrism, saying: 'The sign of Christ unto life eternal. Amen.' "[53]

Thus the anointing and the signing have been combined.

The next witness, *Ordo Romanus XI*, probably reflects the practice of the latter part of the sixth century. After baptism with its presbyteral anointing the infants are brought to the bishop:

"And being vested, they are arranged in order as their names are written, in a circle, and the pontiff makes a prayer over them, confirming them with an invocation of the sevenfold grace of the Holy Spirit. When the prayer has been said, he makes the sign of the cross with his thumb and chrism on the forehead of each one saying: 'In the Name of the Father and of the Son and of the Holy Ghost. Peace be to thee.' And they reply: 'Amen.' Great care must be taken that this is not neglected, because it is at that point that every baptism is confirmed and justification made for the name of Christianity. After this they go in to Mass and all the infants receive communion. Care is to be taken lest after they have been baptized they receive any food or suckling before they communicate."[54]

Around the millennium the rite of confirmation is found in that pontifical that serves as the immediate source for all future Roman pontificals, the Romano-Germanic Pontifical.[55] The bishop raises his hand over the heads of all the newly baptized infants (collectively) and prays for the sevenfold gifts of the Holy Spirit. He then makes the sign of the cross with chrism on the forehead of each praying, "I confirm and sign you in the name of the Father, and of the Son, and of the Holy Spirit."[56]

In the Roman Pontifical of the Twelfth Century there is

21

an individual laying on of the hand by the bishop at the beginning of the rite, as the bishop prays, "May the Holy Spirit come down upon you and may the power of the Most High keep you from sin. Amen." After the traditional prayer for the sevenfold gifts, the bishop signs the forehead with chrism using the formula appearing for the first time and that will endure down through the centuries: "I sign thee with the sign of the cross and I confirm thee with the chrism of salvation. In the name of the Father and of the Son and of the Holy Spirit. Amen."[57]

By the end of the thirteenth century, further changes in the rite are found in the Pontifical of William Durandus. The individual hand-laying is dropped, and the bishop has a collective imposition (of both hands) before the prayer for the sevenfold gifts. The bishop then anoints the forehead of each candidate with chrism, using the thumb of his right hand. Then Durandus adds, "And then he gives him a light blow (*alapa*) on the cheek, saying, 'Peace be with you.' "[58] This addition represents, as was said, a stage in the journey of seeing confirmation less as part of the initiatory rite (symbolized by a welcoming kiss of peace) and more as a separate gesture of preparing for the struggles of the Christian life (symbolized by a blow on the cheek). It is interesting to note that this *alapa* is also used in Durandus's Pontifical for the blessing of a new soldier.[59]

The first "official" edition of the Roman Pontifical appeared in 1596. The Roman Pontifical of Clement VIII was the first in the history of the church to be constituted as the unique model, abrogating all other previous pontificals of the Latin church.[60] It follows the confirmation pattern as found in the Pontifical of William Durandus.

The first mention of imposing the hand during the anointing comes in the eighteenth century with the Pontifical of Benedict XIII. It is found in the Appendix and covers the case of confirmation of only one person.[61] In time this custom of laying the hand on the head of the confirmand during the anointing became the common practice in the West, not only when confirming one person only, but also for the more common occurrence, the confirming of groups. It is interesting, however, that the rubric calling for the hand to be laid on the head of the confirmand during the anointing never did enter the Pontifical for the rite of confirming groups. Curiously, it was there for the rite of confirming one person only, and it was in the Roman Ritual from 1925 onward where it was applied to the case of confirmation being conferred by a priest who had received delegation from a bishop.[62]

At first sight it might be argued that these liturgical books give witness to a shift of emphasis from a laying on of hands to anointing as the essential gesture in the liturgy of confirmation. Some do hold this position, yet others would counter that the very act of anointing was seen as containing in itself a laying on of the hand. Others would see the imposition of hands preserved in the collective imposition at the beginning of the rite.

A PRACTICE SEEKING A THEORY

Our investigation has been limited to the historical development of confirmation in the West. The Christian East has not been considered since it had no real bearing on the Roman rite. It is regrettable that Gallican "confirmation" with its Eastern borrowings did not influence the Roman rite more than it did; it could have enriched the Roman practice with Eastern elements.

From an early time in history there appeared two different mind sets: one in the West and one in the East.[63] The matter is put extremely well by G. Kretschmar:

"Already by the fourth century we encounter a peculiarity of the Latin baptismal theology as opposed to the Easterners, a peculiarity which will determine the way of baptism in the West in the following centuries. Among the Greeks the capacity grew ever stronger to view the various rites of baptism looking out from a central point as it were, the baptismal bath, as the unfolding of the one baptism according to the laws of the divine economy of salvation. Ambrose is able to understand the individual partial actions of baptism only as divinely established rites which follow one another in consecutive order and whose respective function must be kept separate from one another. The circle, or even the ellipse, corresponds to the structure of the Greek thinking; the straight line corresponds to the structure of the Latin thinking. For this reason among the Greeks baptism in the fullness of its rites remained a unity; among the Latins it could come back to a unity only when the consignation had been separated from baptism and become a 'sacrament' of its own."[64]

In the straight line of the Latin thinking the earliest understanding of the postbaptismal ceremonies was christological in tone, at the expense of the development of pneumatology. The complementary ceremonies surrounding baptism look back to the water-bath and explicate the initiates' participation in Christ. For Ambrose the anointing immediately following the water-bath is christological in terms of regeneration and forgiveness. The formula accompanying the anointing is: "God the Father Almighty, who has regenerated you by water and the Holy Spirit, and has forgiven you your sins, himself anoint you unto eternal life."[65] This anointing for Ambrose is, then, an unfolding of the meaning of the baptismal bath.[66] The giving of the Holy Spirit is for him intimately tied to the consignation, the "spiritual seal," which takes place after the foot-washing and the reception of the white garment. Whether this ceremony signifying the communication of the Holy Spirit employed chrism is uncertain; some authors feel it probably did.[67]

When one turns to the Eastern Fathers it is impossible to identify an element of the initiation ceremony that today would be called confirmation, because they viewed initiation as a whole as being imbedded in pneumatology. The earliest Eastern initiation theology is that found in the Syriac and Armenian sources of the first four centuries. Here initiation is not modeled on the Pauline "death-mysticism" of dying and rising with Christ, but on the Jordan event where Christ is born of water and the Spirit. The baptismal action is based on John 3: "Truly, truly, I say to you, unless one is born of water and the Spirit, he cannot enter the kingdom of God. That which is born of the flesh is flesh, and that which is born of the Spirit is spirit" (vss. 5–6). It looks back to Genesis 1 and 2. In this sense it may be called a Spirit-centered "genesis-mysticism."[68]

Speaking of the fourth century H. Riley writes: "When Cyril says that the neophyte received the Holy Spirit in the anointing after baptism, he is thinking 'inclusively' and not 'exclusively,' for in the Eastern fathers, the communication of the Holy Spirit is seen in the totality of Christian Initiation. Hence, their thinking does not admit of too much application of a more linear Western mode of thought."[69]

The trinitarian heresies of the fourth century brought with them a greater need to establish and then also to defend the divinity of the Holy Spirit, which furthered the cause of the identification of chrism with proof that the Holy Spirit was consubstantial with the Father and the Son. But any interpretation of any of the individual ritual actions was viewed in terms of the totality of Christian initiation. If one aspect of the process was what would today be called confirmation, that aspect would have legitimately been understood only within the total organic reality of initiation. Once the ritual communication of the Holy Spirit is taken out of that total context, the door is open for misinterpretation. As we have seen, that is precisely what happened. Thus, the reality that the scholastics of the twelfth and thirteenth centuries inherited as "confirmation" was a very different thing from the early church's sealing with the Spirit, leading to participation in the paschal eucharist.

The scholastics turned their attention to understanding the sacrament of confirmation and specifying precisely its effects. They did this, however, using the terminology of previous writers, particularly of Faustus. His ideas of an increase of grace and strengthening for battle were taken for granted, presented, and then thought through anew. Thus the understanding of confirmation presumed and then developed by the scholastics was not the older image of initiating a person into the church, but rather the act of "gracing" more deeply a person already baptized.

This understanding is true for the most important scholastic writer on confirmation, Thomas Aquinas.[70] Thomas's ideas of a growth and a strength given in confirmation stem from his quotations of the pseudo-Pope Melchiades, which in reality are the words of Faustus. In the framework of Thomas's dominant analogy between bodily growth and spiritual growth, confirmation enters as the Christian sacrament of spiritual maturity. The grace confirmation gives is an increase of the grace already present through baptism, which caused grace initially. In confirmation one receives a specific grace "for growing and maturing in holiness."[71] He says that confirmation "gives the Holy Spirit to the baptized for their strengthening just as it was given to the apostles on the day of Pentecost, and as it was given to the baptized through the imposition of hands by the apostles."[72] A further giving of the Spirit is the purpose of the sacrament: "In this sacrament the fullness of the

Holy Spirit is given for the spiritual strength which is proper to maturity."[73] Maturity is described as preparation for a spiritual battle outside one's self against the enemies of the faith. In baptism a "power is received for performing those things which pertain to one's own salvation in so far as one lives for oneself."[74]

For Aquinas, confirmation, like baptism and holy order, imprints a character, which is a "certain kind of participation in the priesthood of Christ."[75] Due to the hierarchical thinking of his time, he took the sacramental character of order as the prime analogue. In this he differed from Augustine, who began with the character imprinted by baptism. In his treatment of the sacraments in general, Aquinas likens the character of confirmation to that of baptism, by which one is given the power to receive all the other sacraments.[76] Later on, in dealing specifically with the character of confirmation, he differentiates the two characters: "Through the sacrament of confirmation a man is given spiritual power for activity that is different from that for which power is given in baptism. For in baptism power is received for performing those things which pertain to one's own salvation in so far as one lives for oneself. In confirmation a person receives power for engaging in the spiritual battle against the enemies of the faith."[77]

Modern theologians hesitate to accept such an individualistic concept of baptism. Still, Aquinas's thinking in this area of confirmation and its relation to baptism totally dominated the theological arena for centuries. It is unfortunate that he did not have at his disposal the resources available to modern liturgical scholarship—editions of early sacramentaries, ordinals, etc. Due to this deficiency he shared the medieval period's lack of familiarity with liturgical history, which caused him to treat confirmation in an incomplete way.

The treatment of confirmation by the Council of Florence (1438–1445) follows Thomas Aquinas almost verbatim.[78] A key statement of the Council reads: "In place of that imposition of hand (of Acts 8), confirmation is given in the church."[79] The text is not an attempt to see "confirmation" in the Acts of the Apostles, but an assertion that the sacramental reality today called "confirmation" accomplishes that which the imposition of hands accomplished in apostolic times. Aquinas stated that the only minister of confirmation was the bishop; the statement of Florence changed this to the bishop's being the "ordinary minister."

A century later, the Council of Trent (1545–1563) spoke in the cultural milieu of the Reformation. It wanted to defend the sacramental character of confirmation against the reformers who had denied it: "If anyone says that the confirmation of baptized persons is a useless ceremony and not rather a true and proper sacrament; or that at one time it meant nothing other than a certain catechesis by which those nearing adolescence explained the basis of their faith before the church: let him be anathema."[80] The reformers felt that the importance of baptism had been weakened by attributing too much to the subsidiary rites such as hand-laying and anointing.

A second canon of Trent states that it is not injurious to the Holy Spirit to use chrism.[81] There was no attempt here to define the essential rite of confirmation. David Greenstock writes: "The Fathers were content with a condemnation of the heretical doctrines concerning the use of chrism. Consequently, the necessity of the anointing as the essential matter is not defined, nor is there any clear statement as to the efficacy of this element in the rite."[82] The third and last canon echoes the Council of Florence and states that the bishop is the "ordinary" minister of the sacrament.[83]

In the eighteenth century, Pope Benedict XIV states in his encyclical *Ex quo primum* that the Greeks do not have the imposition of hands in their confirmation ceremony, only the anointing, but we should not deduce from this that they do not have the sacrament of confirmation.[84] The point in common for both East and West is the use of chrism.

At the end of the following century we find the letter *Abrogata* of Pope Leo XIII to the archbishop of Marseilles dated June 22, 1897. This letter served as the immediate source for the 1917 Code of Canon Law concerning the age for confirmation and first communion. The pope approves the practice of conferring confirmation before first communion. He argues that all the faithful need the grace given in confirmation, even from their youth, because it better prepares them to receive the eucharist.[85] In spite of his plea the practice of placing confirmation after first eucharist rather than before continued in most dioceses throughout the world.

The 1917 Code of Canon Law prescribes that confirmation be conferred by the imposition of the hand with the anointing of the forehead.[86] As to the age of the confirmand it states: "Although the administration of the sacrament of confirmation should preferably be postponed in the Latin Church till about the seventh year of age, nevertheless it can be conferred before that age if the infant is in danger of death or if its administration seems to the minister justified for good and serious reasons."[87] While this canon may not be used to argue for the practice of infant confirmation, nevertheless, responses from the Roman congregations during the twentieth century definitely reveal a desire to lower the age. In spite of prevalent practice to the contrary, the ideal urged in the legislation was to maintain the traditional order of the initiation sacraments: baptism, confirmation, eucharist.

The Second Vatican Council said very little about confirmation. By far the most important thing it did state was: "The rite of confirmation is also to be revised in order that the intimate connection of this sacrament with the whole of Christian initiation may stand out more clearly."[88] Anything else the council has to say about confirmation must be judged in the light of that overarching statement, which localized confirmation in its proper setting. What was said in the *Constitution on the Church* shows the influence of Aquinas and the medieval tradition: "By the sacrament of confirmation the faithful are more perfectly bound to the church and are endowed with the special strength of the Holy Spirit. Hence they are, as true witnesses of Christ, more strictly obliged to spread the faith by word and deed."[89] The final place where the council spoke of confirmation was in the *Decree on the Catholic Eastern Churches.* The traditional Eastern practice of allowing priests to "confirm" was upheld, using chrism blessed by their patriarch or bishop.[90]

CONCLUSION

From our perusal of the historical development of confirmation we can conclude that no other sacrament has had such a checkered history and that no other sacrament has been so subject to a search for a meaning. If one seeks a single word to describe the history of confirmation perhaps the most precise would be "disintegration"; disintegration of the unity of the rite itself and of the significance of that rite. The hallmark of the early church was unity: one Lord, one faith, one baptism. Entrance into the church was marked by that unity and specified that unity; becoming a Christian meant living in and by the Spirit, the principle of unity. The infant church came into being through the Pentecost event, and that event constituted the infant church's most vibrant recollection of initiation, an event not of water but of Spirit. It was living in the Holy

Spirit, in the context of a Spirit-filled community, that gave continuity and sense to the Christian life. All this was celebrated at the outset of the journey in the Spirit by the sacraments of initiation.

Down through the centuries the problem has been basically the same: to treat the various moments of the initiation process in isolation rather than as constituting a unity, incorporation into Christ. Today, from the vantage point of twenty years after the Second Vatican Council, we ask ourselves if the liturgical reforms of the new rite of confirmation and of the rite of blessing of oil and chrism have failed or succeeded in preserving that unity.

NOTES

1. See Oscar Cullmann, *Baptism in the New Testament* (SCM Press, London 1950), p. 9–22.

2. See W. F. Flemington, *The New Testament Doctrine of Baptism* (SPCK, London 1964), p. 29.

3. Aidan Kavanagh, *The Shape of Baptism: The Rite of Christian Initiation* (Pueblo, New York 1978), p. 25.

4. Ignace de la Potterie and Stanislaus Lyonnet, *The Christian Lives by the Spirit* (Alba House, Staten Island 1971), p. 35.

5. James D. G. Dunn, *Baptism in the Holy Spirit* (SCM Press, London 1970), p. 224.

6. See Geoffrey Wainwright, *Christian Initiation* (John Knox Press, Richmond 1969), p. 13.

7. See Richard J. Dillon and Joseph A. Fitzmyer, "Acts of the Apostles" in Raymond Brown (ed.), *The Jerome Biblical Commentary* (Prentice-Hall, Englewood Cliffs, N.J. 1968), p. 185.

8. Reginald Fuller, "Christian Initiation in the New Testament" in *Made, Not Born* (University of Notre Dame Press, Notre Dame 1976), p. 14.

9. Rudolf Schnackenburg, *Baptism in the Thought of St. Paul* (Herder and Herder, New York 1964), p. 91.

10. See Thomas Marsh, "A Study of Confirmation," *Irish Theological Quarterly* 39 (1972), p. 161.

11. Raymond Brown, "We Profess One Baptism for the Forgiveness of Sins," *Worship* 40 (1966), p. 265.

12. See J. D. G. Dunn, "Spirit, Holy" in Colin Brown (ed.), *The New International Dictionary of New Testament Theology* (Zondervan, Grand Rapids 1975), Vol. 3, pp. 699–700.

13. See De la Potterie and Lyonnet, pp. 85–90.

14. Ibid., pp. 79–143. Also see Reginald Fuller, p. 25.

15. See Schnackenburg, pp. 162–166.

16. See J. Ysebaert, *Greek Baptismal Terminology: Its Origins and Early Development* (Dekker & Van de Vegt N.V., Nijmegen 1962), pp. 182–426. A readable survey is found in Jean Daniélou, *The Bible and the Liturgy* (University of Notre Dame Press, Notre Dame 1956), pp. 54–69.

17. "Accipe signaculum Doni Spiritus Sancti."

18. G. W. H. Lampe, *The Seal of the Spirit* (SPCK, London 1967), p. 309.

19. Ibid., p. 7.

20. Ernest Evans (ed.), *Tertullian's Homily on Baptism* (SPCK, London 1964), p. 15.

21. See E. C. Whitaker, *Documents of the Baptismal Liturgy* (SPCK, London 1970), pp. 2–7.

22. Ibid., p. 6. Whitaker translates the penultimate phrase as "and sealing him on the forehead." The manuscript traditions give both *consignans* in the Latin and *sphragizein* in the Greek. See Bernard Botte (ed.), *La Tradition Apostolique de Saint Hippolyte* (Aschendorf, Münster 1963), p. 54.

23. There will be slight modifications of this pattern; for example, the anointing and the sealing will be combined.

24. Whitaker, pp. 229–230.

25. This translation is that of Gabriele Winkler, "Confirmation or Chrismation? A Study in Comparative Liturgy," *Worship* 58 (1984), pp. 9–10. An excellent study of this canon

may be found in L. A. Van Buchem, *L'Homélie Pseudo-Eusébienne de Pentecôte* (Drukkerij Gebr. Janssen N.V., Nijmegen 1967), pp. 95–110.

26. Winkler, pp. 11–12.

27. Ibid., p. 13.

28. Ibid., pp. 2–8.

29. For the critical edition of this homily, see Van Buchem, pp. 40–44. I am indebted for insights into Faustus to Eugene M. Finnegan, "The Origins of Confirmation in the Western Church"; unpublished doctoral dissertation: Theological Faculty of Trier, Germany, 1970.

30. Gregory Dix, *The Theology of Confirmation in Relation to Baptism* (Dacre, London 1946), p. 26.

31. "Ergo spiritus sanctus qui super aquas baptismi salutifero descendit inlapsu, in fonte plenitudinem tribuit ad innocentiam, in confirmatione augumentum praestat ad gratiam, quia in hoc mundo tota aetate uicturis inter inuisibiles hostes et pericula gradiendum est. In baptismo regeneramur ad uitam, post baptismum confirmamur ad pugnam. In baptismo abluimur post baptismum roboramur." Van Buchem, p. 41.

32. See E. H. Davenport, *The False Decretals* (Blackwell, Oxford 1916), pp. 92–97.

33. Irenaeus, *Adversus Haereses* III, 18, 3.

34. See Louis Ligier, *La Confirmation: Sens et conjoncture oecuménique hier et aujourd'hui* (Beauchesne, Paris 1973), pp. 160–161.

35. Bernard Botte, "Postbaptismal Anointing in the Ancient Patriarchate of Antioch," in Jacob Vellian (ed.), *Studies on Syrian Baptismal Rites*, The Syrian Churches Series 6 (CMS Press, Kottayam 1973), p. 71.

36. Letter 159; PL 54, 1138–1139.

37. Gregory the Great, *Epistula XI* 52 in L. Hartmann (ed.), *Monumenta Germaniae Historica* 2 (1899), p. 325.

38. See J. Macdonald, "Imposition of Hands in the Letters of

Innocent I," *Studia Patristica II* (Akademie-Verlag, Berlin 1957), pp. 49–53.

39. The most enlightening study in this area is J. D. C. Fisher, *Christian Initiation: Baptism in the Medieval West* (SPCK, London 1965). Key to his thesis is Chapter three, "Christian Initiation in Gaul and Germany," pp. 47–77. A recent study corroborating Fisher's position is Joseph L. Levesque, "The Theology of the Postbaptismal Rites in the Seventh and Eighth Century Gallican Church," *Ephemerides Liturgicae* 95 (1981), pp. 3–43.

40. See P. M. Gy, "Quamprimum. Note sur le baptême des enfants," *La Maison-Dieu* 32 (1952), pp. 124–128.

41. Letter 241; PL 182, 434.

42. Winkler, p. 7.

43. Leonel L. Mitchell, *Baptismal Anointing* (SPCK, London 1966), p. 125.

44. See Fisher, p. 64.

45. Letter 134. Fisher, pp. 60–61.

46. Fisher, p. 61.

47. Whitaker, p. 204.

48. See H. Denzinger and A. Schönmetzer, *Enchiridion Symbolorum* (Herder, New York 1976), no. 812. This work will be abbreviated DS.

49. Ibid., no. 1730.

50. Ibid., no. 1734.

51. See P. M. Gy, "Histoire liturgique du sacrement de confirmation," *La Maison-Dieu* 58 (1959) 141.

52. Whitaker, pp. 166–196. For an invaluable chronological listing of all the confirmation formulas in the Western church see Estanislau M. Llopart, "Les Fórmules de la Confirmació en el Pontifical Romà," *Liturgica* 2, Scripta et documenta 10 (Montserrat, 1958), pp. 121–180.

53. "Signum Christi in vitam aeternam." Whitaker, p. 188.

54. Ibid., pp. 203–204.

55. Cyrille Vogel (ed.), *Le Pontifical Romano-Germanique du dixième siècle,* 2 vols., Studi e Testi 226, 227 (Biblioteca Apostolica Vaticana, Vatican City 1963).

56. Ibid., vol. 2, p. 109.

57. Michel Andrieu, *Le Pontifical Romain au moyen-age:* Tome I: *Le Pontifical Romain du XIIe siècle,* Studi e Testi 86 (Biblioteca Apostolica Vaticana, Vatican City 1938), p. 247.

58. Ibid., Tome III: *Le Pontifical de Guillaume Durand,* Studi e Testi 88 (Biblioteca Apostolica Vaticana, Vatican City 1940), pp. 333–334.

59. Ibid., pp. 447–450.

60. See Gerard Austin, "The Essential Rite of Confirmation and Liturgical Tradition," *Ephemerides Liturgicae* 86 (1972) pp. 214–224.

61. This 1725 *Pontifical of Benedict XIII* is nowhere to be found today. Our information comes from the testimony of Catalani: Joseph Catalani, *Pontificale in tres partes distributum Clementis VIII ac Urbani VIII,* vol. 1 (Paris 1850), p. 5.

62. *Rituale Romanum* Tit. 3, Cap. 1, nos. 1, 3; Tit. 3, cap. 2, no. 6.

63. There are two recent studies that throw remarkable light on the initiatory practices of the early Christian East: Augustin Mouhana, *Les rites de l'initiation dans l'église Maronite,* Orientalia Christiana Analecta 212 (Pontificium Institutum Studiorum Orientalium, Rome 1978); Gabriele Winkler, *Das Armenische Initiationsrituale,* Orientalia Christiana Analecta 217 (Pontificium Institutum Studiorum Orientalium, Rome 1982).

64. Georg Kretschmar, "Die Geschichte des Taufgottesdienstes in der alten Kirche" in *Leitourgia. Handbuch des evangelischen Gottesdienstes 5* (J. Stauda Verlag, Kassel 1970), p. 236.

65. Whitaker, p. 130. This same formula is passed on in the West through the Gelasian Sacramentary; Whitaker, p. 188.

66. See Hugh M. Riley, *Christian Initiation: A Comparative Study of the Interpretation of the Baptismal Liturgy in the Mystagogical Writings of Cyril of Jerusalem, John Chrysostom, Theodore of Mopsuestia, and Ambrose of Milan* (Catholic University of America Press, Washington, D.C. 1974), p. 391.

67. For example Leonel L. Mitchell, *Baptismal Anointing* (SPCK, London 1966), p. 90.

68. See Winkler, p. 444. See also her "Eine bemerkenswerte Stelle in armenischen Glaubensbekenntnis: Credimus et in Spiritum Sanctum qui descendit in Jordanem proclamavit missum," *Oriens Christianus* 63 (1979) 130–162; and her "The Original Meaning of the Prebaptismal Anointing and its Implications," *Worship* 52 (1978), pp. 24–45.

69. Riley, p. 399.

70. Aquinas wrote of confirmation in four places: *Scriptum super libros Sententiarum* 4.7; *Summa contra gentiles* 4.60; *De articulis fidei et Ecclesiae sacramentis ad archiepiscopum Panormitanum; Summa theologiae* 3.72.

71. *Summa theologiae* III, q. 72, art. 7 ad 1: "Et ideo gratia gratum faciens, non solum datur ad remissionem culpae, sed etiam ad augmentum et firmitatem justitiae. Et sic confertur in hoc sacramento." The translations of Thomas are my own.

72. Ibid., III, q. 72, art. 8.

73. Ibid., III, q. 72, art. 2.

74. Ibid., III, q. 72, art. 5.

75. Ibid., III, q. 63, art. 3.

76. Ibid., III, q. 63, art. 6.

77. Ibid., III, q. 72, art. 5.

78. From his *De articulis fidei et Ecclesiae sacramentis ad archiepiscopum Panormitanum.*

79. DS, no. 1318.

80. DS, no. 1628.

81. DS, no. 1629.

82. David L. Greenstock, "The Problem of Confirmation" in *The Thomist Reader: Texts and Studies* (Thomist Press, Washington, D.C. 1957), p. 125.

83. DS, no. 1630.

84. Benedict XIV, *Ex quo primum,* no. 50. See P. Gasparri, *Codicis Iuris Canonici Fontes II* (Typis Polyglottis Vaticanis, Vatican City 1925), p. 507.

85. See Gasparri, vol. 3, p. 634. For a helpful discussion of this letter of Leo XIII, see Bernard Botte, "A propos de la confirmation," *Nouvelle Revue Theologique* 88 (1966), pp. 848–852.

86. Canon 780 (1917 Code). The 1983 Code will be treated in the next chapter, "The New Rite of Confirmation."

87. Canon 788 (1917 Code).

88. *Sacrosanctum Concilium,* no. 71. *Documents on the Liturgy 1963-1979* (Liturgical Press, Collegeville 1982), no. 71.

89. *Lumen Gentium,* no. 11. Austin Flannery (ed.), *Vatican Council II: The Conciliar and Post Conciliar Documents* (Costello, Northport, N.Y. 1981), p. 361.

90. *Orientalium Ecclesiarum,* no. 13; Flannery, p. 446.

The Reforms

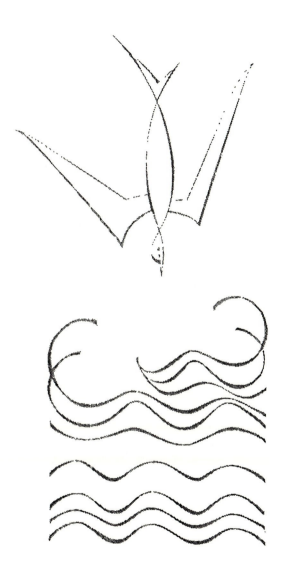

Chapter Two

The New Rite of Confirmation

The *Rite of Confirmation* is the English text of the Latin *Ordo Confirmationis*, which was promulgated on August 15, 1971, by the Apostolic Constitution of Paul VI, *Divinae Consortium Naturae*.[1] The Latin typicum is a document of forty-nine pages containing: the Apostolic Constitution; Introduction [1–19]; Chapter One: Rite of Confirmation Within Mass [20–33]; Chapter Two: Rite of Confirmation Outside Mass [34–49]; Chapter Three: Rite of Confirmation by a Minister Who Is Not a Bishop [50–51]; Chapter Four: Confirmation of a Person in Danger of Death [52–56]; and Chapter Five: Texts for the Celebration of Confirmation [57–65]. The rite is to be viewed as a part of the whole process of initiation and thus should be studied in conjunction with *Ordo Baptismi Parvulorum* (1969)[2] and *Ordo Initiationis Christianae Adultorum* (1972).[3] From the point of view of all three documents, it would have been better had the *Rite of Christian Initiation of Adults* appeared first. Aidan Kavanagh observes:

"The spirit and principles contained in the full rites of adult initiation are operative throughout the other initiatory rites: the former subordinate the latter as soul subordinates body, as function subordinates form. In the most practical way, therefore, the full rites of adult initiation give shape, articulation, and fundamental continuity of meaning to all the other rites which constitute the Roman initiatory economy."[4]

The new *Rite of Confirmation* attempts first and foremost to carry out Vatican II's mandate that this sacrament should express its intimate connection with the whole initiation process: "The rite of confirmation is also to be revised in order that the intimate connection of this sacrament with the whole of Christian initiation may stand out more clearly."[5] This connection is the key to resolving many of the problems touching the meaning of confirmation. In the Apostolic Constitution, Paul VI states: "The faithful are born anew by baptism, strengthened by the sacrament of confirmation, and finally are sustained by the food of eternal life in the eucharist."[6] Time and again this traditional ordering of the sacraments of initiation is given in the revised rites. Paul VI goes so far as to say that the interdependence among the sacraments of initiation is the very key to interpreting the constitutive elements of confirmation: "The link between confirmation and the other sacraments of initiation is shown forth more clearly not only by closer association of these sacraments but also by the rite and words by which confirmation is conferred."[7] This close link is best fostered by respecting the traditional ordering of the three initiation sacraments (baptism, confirmation, eucharist), because, as will be seen, confirmation is a completion of baptism and in turn leads to participation in the eucharist.

THE ESSENTIAL RITE OF CONFIRMATION
The Apostolic Constitution approaches the difficult and complicated problem of specifying the essential rite of confirmation.[8] Since the twelfth and thirteenth centuries, the essential rite is what has been called the "matter" and "form" of a sacrament. It was a thirteenth-century theologian, Hugh of Saint Cher, who first put the two terms "matter" and "form" together with hylomorphic meaning: that is, "matter" as the determinable principle, "form" as the determining.[9] But both the Apostolic Constitution and the *Rite of Confirmation*

avoid the terms "matter" and "form." The terminology is used only indirectly in the Apostolic Constitution, where it is a question of quoting the Council of Florence as it speaks of the matter of the sacrament.[10]

From the early centuries of the church there was confusion or divided opinion over just what constituted confirmation. One might say that there was no real answer to this question in the earliest centuries because confirmation was not yet perceived as a sacrament separate from baptism. As time passed, however, the West seemed to favor the laying on of hands while the East favored the anointing. Yet the Apostolic Constitution says: "From what we have recalled, it is clear that in the administration of confirmation in the East and the West, though in different ways, the most important place was occupied by the anointing, which in a certain way represents the apostolic laying on of hands."[11] This statement is a bit puzzling in the light of all the historical evidence that stresses the laying on of hands.[12]

There are, in fact, two laying on of hands involved in the *Rite of Confirmation:* (1) the general or global imposition over all the candidates that the bishop performs before the anointing as he says the prayer for the sevenfold gifts of the Spirit [25]; and (2) the individual imposition on each candidate as the anointing takes place [27]. In certain periods of the church's history, many theologians viewed the first, the global imposition, as the essential rite of the sacrament. But this opinion was ruled out by Paul VI in the Apostolic Constitution:

"Although the laying of hands on the candidates, which is done with the prescribed prayer before the anointing, does not belong to the essence of the sacramental rite, it is nevertheless to be held in high esteem, in that it contributes to the integral perfection of that rite and to a clearer understanding of the sacrament. It is evident that this preceding laying on of hands differs from the laying on of the hand by which the anointing is done on the forehead."[13]

This negative stance toward the global imposition arises from the context of the frequent questions received over the past hundred years by the Holy See from bishops concerned about candidates for confirmation who would arrive late, missing the first imposition of hands. While such late arrival was not to be encouraged, the candidates were to be considered validly confirmed.[14]

Pastoral questions lead one to understand, then, why distinctions arise between what belongs to the "essential rite" of confirmation and what belongs to the "integrity" of the rite ("integral perfection," as Paul VI puts it). Yet, stressing such distinctions might run the risk of flirting with a minimalistic approach to sacramental theology. The pinpointing of precise moments in worship has in the past led to unfortunate arguments such as the one between East and West over the epiclesis and the "moment of consecration."

The 1917 Code of Canon Law prescribed that confirmation be conferred by the imposition of the hand with the anointing of the forehead,[15] which was interpreted by canonists as referring principally neither to the imposition of the hand nor to the anointing but to "the one act by which the hand is imposed and the chrism applied at one and the same time."[16] In 1971, Paul VI worded his intent with extreme precision by stating in the Apostolic Constitution: "The Sacrament of Confirmation is conferred through the anointing with chrism on the forehead, which is done by the laying on of the hand, and through the words: 'Accipe Signaculum Doni Spiritus Sancti.' "[17] Yet when one looks at the text of the Ordo itself there is no mention of any laying on of the hand during the anointing, an action found since the Pontifical of Benedict XIII in 1725.[18]

A great deal of confusion resulted. Some thought it to be a misprint, an omission of some sort.[19] Most bishops went right along celebrating the sacrament as they had always done, imposing the hand while anointing the forehead. Some bishops petitioned Rome for a clarification and finally, on June 9, 1972, a response was made by the Pontifical Commission for Interpreting the Decrees of Vatican II with the approbation of Paul VI.[20] Should the minister of confirmation extend his hand over the head of the confirmand while anointing? No. Did the anointing with the thumb alone suffice? Yes: the anointing so carried out sufficiently manifests the imposition of the hand.[21] This response is incredible, and certainly one that from an anthropological point of view does violence to the authenticity of the sign of the imposition of hands. The imposition of a thumb simply is not an imposition of hands. At a time when the venerable gesture of the laying on of hands is becoming so important (for example, in healing services), one can only lament such a response.[22]

As to the formula—the words of the rite by which the Holy Spirit is given—Paul VI made a significant change. He reached back in both time and space, by adopting a Byzantine formula that probably had been in use in the East since the fifth century: "Accipe Signaculum Doni Spiritus Sancti."[23] This formula combines two New Testament passages: Ephesians 1:13, where Paul writes that in Christ "you were sealed with the promised Holy Spirit"; and Acts 2:38, where Peter in his Pentecost sermon urges his hearers to be baptized, "and you shall receive the gift of the Holy Spirit."

Just how to translate the new formula into English proved to be a difficult task that resulted in two years of tension between Rome and the International Committee on English in the Liturgy (ICEL).[24] The first ICEL translation was: "Receive the seal of the Holy Spirit, the Gift of the Father." ICEL argued that the origin of the gift in the Father should be mentioned; that while the Son was not mentioned, his active mission of the Holy Spirit was implicit in the whole rite; that the formula expressed the external mission of the Holy Spirit and not the eternal procession of the Holy Spirit from Father and Son. Rome refused to approve the ICEL translation, however, and finally settled the matter by insisting on: "Be sealed with the Gift of the Holy Spirit."[25] This final English translation would seem preferable for two reasons. First, it avoids the problem of not explicitly mentioning the Son while mentioning the Father. Second, it avoids the problem of the seal being an intermediate element; the confirmand does not receive the seal of the Holy Spirit but is directly sealed with the gift, who is the Holy Spirit.

The original suggestion to use the ancient Byzantine formula came from Dom Bernard Botte.[26] On first view its adoption by the West appears to be a laudable ecumenical gesture, but a closer look reveals what some would call a false ecumenism, because the formula has been removed from its total context. As borrowed and used by the new rite, the formula lacks the epicletic prayers that accompany it and give it meaning in the Byzantine context.[27]

In his Apostolic Constitution, Paul VI states that the receiving of the Holy Spirit as a gift concerns the very essence of the rite of confirmation.[28] This gift was given in a special way on the day of Pentecost, and from then on the Spirit-filled church has brought new members into this life by preaching that leads to baptism. "Those who believed the Apostles' preaching were then baptized and they too received 'the gift of the Holy Spirit' (Acts 2:38)."[29] But then the Apostolic Constitution adds a position that seems to surpass, if not contradict, the biblical evidence: "From that time on the Apostles, in fulfillment of Christ's wish, imparted to the neophytes the gift of the Spirit, by the laying on of hands to complete the grace of baptism."[30] One wonders just where such a wish of Christ was ever expressed. Multiple patterns of initiation combinations can be found in the Acts of the Apostles, but none sets up a standard pattern to be followed faithfully. None offers a proof that the laying on of hands completes water baptism.[31] Some Scripture scholars argue that there is no evidence in the Acts justifying the positing of a regular ceremony whereby the Spirit was conferred by the laying on of hands. It seems far more accurate to say that at first both tradition and St. Paul speak of a single rite of initiation called "baptism," from its fundamental and most impressive action, the water-bath.[32]

THE MINISTER OF CONFIRMATION

The bishop is the minister *par excellence* of all the sacraments of initiation.[33] The new rite applies that principle to confirmation:

"The original minister of confirmation is the bishop. Ordinarily the sacrament is administered by the bishop so that there will be a more evident relationship to the first pouring forth of the Holy Spirit on the day of Pentecost"[7]. "When confirmation is given by a minister who is not a bishop, whether by concession of the general law or by special indult of the Apostolic See, he should mention in the homily that the bishop is the original minister of the sacrament. He should explain why priests receive the faculty to confirm from the law or by an indult of the Apostolic See" [18].

In 1774, an Instruction of the Congregation for the Propagation of the Faith decreed that priests of the Latin rite who confirm should not only provide such an explanation, but that they should read aloud and in the vernacular the document which gave them the power to confirm.[34] The logical argument for the primacy of the bishop as the minister of the sacrament is based on the outpouring of the Holy Spirit on the apostles at Pentecost. Today the bishops, functioning as the successors to the apostles, impart the same Spirit to the confirmands. Paul VI went so far as to even equate the grace of confirmation with the grace of Pentecost.[35]

The bishop's presidency offers a preeminent sign or manifestation of the local church or diocese. According to the rite,

"attention should be paid to the festive and solemn character of the liturgical service, especially its significance for the local church. It is appropriate for all the candidates to be assembled for a common celebration. The whole people of God, represented by the families and friends of the candidates and by members of the local community, will be invited to take part in the celebration and will express its faith in the fruits of the Holy Spirit" [4].

The norm is confirmation in the context of the parochial eucharistic celebration. The obstacle of the great length of the service due to a large number to be confirmed is now solved by the fact that the bishop may have other priests help him in the celebration. It is a true concelebration, since the associate ministers impose hands along with the bishop during the global imposition of hands, although they do not recite the prayer for the sevenfold gifts; and they anoint the candidates while reciting each time the form, "Be sealed with the Gift of the Holy Spirit" [28].

While any priest not subject to censure or canonical penalty may confirm in danger of death, the normal large-group situation envisions the bishop presiding with associate priests participating. Even in the absence of the bishop certain priests can confirm including "priests who, in virtue of an office which they lawfully hold, baptize an adult or a child old enough for catechesis, or admit a validly baptized adult into full communion with the Church" [7]. Here the question of lapsed Catholics frequently arises. For example, those validly baptized in infancy but never reared as Catholics—can they be confirmed on the occasion of their return to the practice of the faith by the priests mentioned in paragraph 7 of the *Rite of Confirmation?* The Pontifical Commission on the Proper Interpretation of the Decrees of Vatican II declared that they could not.[36] This restriction seems pastorally unfortunate. It would seem most desirable, for example, to confirm such a lapsed Catholic returning to the practice of the faith at the very same time his or her spouse is being confirmed on the occasion of baptism at the completion of the catechumenate or on the occasion of admission into full communion. This is not a rare occurrence on Holy Saturday night in the United States and it is difficult, to say the least, to explain to people that one spouse will be able to be confirmed by a priest, while the other spouse will have to wait until the next time a bishop makes his confirmation rounds. It is hoped that this problem will be solved, at least on the local level, by bishops' free use of the expanded permission to delegate granted by Canon 884 of the 1983 Code: "The diocesan bishop is to administer confirmation personally or see that it is administered by another bishop, but if necessity requires he may give the faculty to administer this sacrament to one or more specified presbyters."

It is interesting that the original committee in charge of drafting the new rite asked general permission for bishops to be able to delegate priests to confirm. The reason was the need to avoid mass confirmations lacking in human dignity. The request was denied.[37] The practical solution in most places has been to relegate the task primarily to auxiliary bishops. However, there is a growing feeling in many places throughout the world that the practice of using auxiliary bishops as "confirming machines" is far from the ideal. It introduces a number of ecclesiological problems. First, the very need to name auxiliary bishops to help the ordinary of the diocese in his work of confirming seems to indicate that the diocese in question is simply too large for a bishop to handle. In this regard it can be said that we do not have too many bishops; we have too few of them! Second, the problem lies with auxiliary bishops themselves. They are an ecclesial anomaly. On the parish level most people feel that their pastor represents the local bishop.[38] An auxiliary bishop's presence at confirmation ceremonies may hang on to the aspect of episcopal involvement, but his presence is not viewed as being necessarily connected with this particular diocese. In the view of most people he could be the bishop of anywhere. His presence simply ensures that the sacramental celebration is carried out by a validly ordained bishop. Thus, the question of the minister of confirmation is at heart a question of ecclesiology.

A final point concerning the minister of confirmation is whether the bishop should be called the "ordinary" or the "original" minister of the sacrament. The confirmation rituals of modern times, as well as the 1917 Code of Canon Law, stated that the ordinary minister of confirmation is solely a bishop,[39] which followed the teaching of the Council of Trent that anathematized those who would extend the term "ordinary minister" from the unique domain of bishops to that of simple priests.[40] However, Vatican II attempted to respect the oriental tradition in this regard. The *Decree on the Catholic Eastern Churches* states: "The established practice with regard to the minister of Confirmation, which has existed among Eastern Christians from ancient times, is to be fully restored. Accordingly priests are able to confer this sacrament, using chrism blessed by their patriarch or bishops."[41] The *Constitution on the Church* calls bishops "the original ministers of Confirmation."[42]

In a session of the Congregation on the Sacraments in preparation for the Council, one of the participants, the Melkite Patriarch Saigh, was very critical of the church's overly Western approach to confirmation. He objected to the bishop being called the ordinary minister and said that in terms of the entire church, East and West, he is rather the "original minister" of the sacrament.[43] These objections were heeded, and the new *Rite of Confirmation* states, "The original minister of confirmation is the bishop" [7].[44] While this may seem like a small point, from an ecumenical point of view it is not. It broadens the perspective and respects the Eastern tradition, as well as the practice of many places in the West over the centuries where initiation by presbyters was viewed as something complete. It is, therefore, disappointing to find that the wording has regressed in the new 1983 Code of Canon Law. There the bishop is not called the original minister, as he is in the new *Rite of Confirmation*, but is called once again the ordinary minister.[45] In this regard it is important to remember that the new code is to be interpreted in the light of the sacramental rites issuing from the Vatican II reform, and not vice versa.

AGE OF THE CONFIRMANDS
To ask "What is the proper age to give confirmation?" is to put the question in the wrong form. The question should be asked, "How long may one delay confirmation?"[46] On May 4, 1774, the Congregation for the Propagation of the Faith issued an Instruction for priests on the missions who were allowed to confirm, and this Instruction was reproduced in all rituals down to that of 1925. A delay until the seventh year is spoken of, but the minister may and should confirm earlier if there is any danger to the child or chance of a valid minister not being available in the future, since the child would thus be deprived of a greater glory in heaven.

In 1897, Pope Leo XIII wrote to the Archbishop of Marseilles that children need the grace given in confirmation even from their tender years, for it prepares them to receive the eucharist.[47] The 1917 Code of Canon Law states: "Although the administration of the sacrament of confirmation should preferably be postponed in the Latin Church until about the seventh year of age, nevertheless it can be conferred before that age if the infant is in danger of death or if its administration seems to the minister justified for good and serious reasons."[48] This approach was inspired by the ancient tradition of the church, a tradition that saw confirmation as the *second step* in the process of Christian initiation. In 1932, the Sacred Congregation for the Sacraments stated that it was more in conformity with the nature of the sacrament of confirmation that children should not come to first communion until they had received confirmation,[49] and in 1952, the Commission for Interpreting the Code of Canon Law denied to local bishops the power to defer confirmation until children were ten years old.[50] This legislation went unheeded in most parts of the world.

The new *Rite of Confirmation* treats the question of age of the candidates and makes a distinction. First, it treats of the obvious case: "Adult catechumens and children who are baptized at an age when they can be catechized should ordinarily be admitted to confirmation and the eucharist at the same time they receive baptism" [11]. This would show the unity of the initiation sacraments and guard the traditional ordering of baptism, confirmation, and eucharist. The *Rite of Christian Initiation of Adults* expresses the theological basis for the practice of placing confirmation and baptism together: "This connection signifies the unity of the paschal mystery, the close relationship between the mission of the Son and the pouring out of the Holy Spirit, and the joint celebration of the sacraments by which the Son and the Spirit come with the Father upon those who are baptized" [34]. Then the *Rite of Confirmation* states, "With regard to children, in the Latin Church the administration of confirmation is generally postponed until about the seventh year" [11]. This represents no change from the practice of the 1917 Code of Canon Law and from modern church legislation, but then a whole new dimension is added by the following qualifying sentence: "For pastoral reasons, however, especially to strengthen in the life of the faithful complete obedience to Christ the Lord in loyal testimony to him, episcopal conferences may choose an age which appears more appropriate, so that the sacrament is conferred after appropriate formation at a more mature age" [11]. This option of delaying the conferring of confirmation to a later age changes the whole focus of the question from the baptismal grace to the baptized person; or, from who we are (those loved gratuitously by God) to what we do (respond to that love).

The bishops of the United States studied this option offered by the new rite to "choose an age which appears more appropriate, so that the sacrament is conferred after appropriate formation at a more mature age" [11] at their plenary session in Atlanta in April 1972. On the recommendation of the Bishops' Committee on Pastoral Research and Practices, the Conference of Bishops voted "that the norm of the *Ordo Confirmationis* be adopted in this country without further modification, saving the right of any Ordinary who might wish to set a later age as normative in his jurisdiction."[51] In practice the norm of the *Ordo*, postponing confirmation until about the seventh year, is rarely the guideline used, since most dioceses in the United States choose to give the sacrament at a later age.

In choosing a later age, an age "which appears more appropriate," one wonders if more is not being demanded for confirmation than is demanded for the apex of Christian initiation, the eucharist itself. While young children are allowed to receive the greatest of all the Christian sacraments, the eucharist, they are denied the right to be confirmed. More important, by delaying the age of confirmation, has not the church turned the sacrament from the purpose for which it was instituted? The church changed confirmation from its original role as the completion and perfection of baptism (and as the gift of the fullness of the Spirit preparing for the reception of the body and blood of Christ) into something totally new: namely, a personal, mature ratification of one's earlier baptism. No sacrament has had such a checkered history as confirmation, and yet tradition shows a constant witness to confirmation as an integral part of the initiation process, as the sacrament that completes the baptismal grace. This is the Roman tradition, and modern theology has produced no new insights or pastoral demands that justify contradicting that venerable tradition.[52]

It is interesting to note that the new 1983 Code of Canon Law makes no mention of conferring confirmation "at a more mature age" as does the *Rite of Confirmation*. It simply states that the sacrament is conferred around the age of discretion, unless episcopal conferences determine another age.[53] It would seem that an earlier as well as a later age could be chosen, and that episcopal conferences could opt even for the practice of infant confirmation, although certainly the thrust of the canon is for the conferral of confirmation at the age of discretion.

SPONSOR FOR CONFIRMATION
The task of the sponsor is described by the new rite of confirmation: "The sponsor brings the candidate to receive the sacrament, presents him to the minister for the anointing, and will later help him to fulfill his baptismal promises faithfully under the influence of the Holy Spirit" [5]. The new rite makes certain changes.

54

The sponsor need no longer be of the same sex as the confirmand, parents are no longer excluded, nor are the baptismal godparents. The rite states: "In view of contemporary pastoral circumstances, it is desirable that the godparent at baptism, if present, also be the sponsor at confirmation; canon 796, no. 1 is abrogated. This change expresses more clearly the relationship between baptism and confirmation and also makes the function and responsibility of the sponsor more effective" [5]. This is a rather strong statement on the close connection between baptism and confirmation. It also helps clarify the role of the confirmation sponsor by using the baptismal godparent as the exemplar.

The *Rite of Christian Initiation of Adults* describes the role of the godparent:

"It is his responsibility to show the catechumen in a friendly way the place of the Gospel in his own life and in society, to help him in doubts and anxieties, to give public testimony for him, and to watch over the progress of his baptismal life. Already a friend before the election, this person exercises his office publicly from the day of election when he gives his testimony about the catechumen before the community. His responsibility remains important when the neophyte has received the sacraments and needs to be helped to remain faithful to his baptismal promises" [43].

Both baptismal godparents and confirmation sponsors reflect the communal nature of Christianity. Newly baptized and newly confirmed Christians learn far more about the lived Christian life from other committed Christians than from lectures on these matters. The godparents and sponsors are important symbols of the love and support of the Christian community.

At the confirmation ceremony the sponsor places his or her right hand on the confirmand's shoulder during the anointing with chrism, replacing an amusing rubric that has been in the *Pontificale Romanum* for the last thousand years. During confirmation sponsors were to hold infant confirmands in their arms. Adult confirmands were to place their foot on the right foot of the sponsor. The rubric can be traced all the way back to the Romano-Germanic Pontifical of the tenth century.[54] Apparently this was a medieval way of symbolizing the support that the sponsor gave the confirmand: holding them in their arms or letting them stand on their foot.

CELEBRATION OF CONFIRMATION

The *Rite of Confirmation* states, "It is the responsibility of the people of God to prepare the baptized for the reception of the sacrament of confirmation" [3]. This statement immediately puts confirmation in a broad, ecclesial context. The guiding principle here is that enunciated in the adult rite: "The initiation of catechumens takes place step by step in the midst of the community of the faithful. Together with the catechumens, the faithful reflect upon the value of the paschal mystery, renew their own conversion, and by their example lead the catechumens to obey the Holy Spirit more generously" [4]. For adult catechumens who are confirmed immediately after their baptism the effects of the catechumenate formation are evident, but the *Rite of Confirmation* says the same is to hold true for those confirmands who were baptized as infants: "The steps of the catechumenate will be appropriately adapted to those who, baptized in infancy, are confirmed only as adults" [3]. This is another proof that all the separate rites that constitute full initiation presume adult initiation to be the governing norm. There confirmation is viewed as one aspect of the spiritual journey that governs the theology of adult initiation. This fact has implications for the catechetical aspects of confirmation programs that are both exciting and challenging. The new rite of adult initiation must be studied, experienced, and contemplated to help throw light on just what should be done in programs of preparation for confirmation. "It is the responsibility of the episcopal conferences to determine more precisely the pastoral means for the preparation of children for confirmation" [12].

The National Catechetical Directory states that due to the great diversity of practice in the United States as to the age of receiving confirmation "it is impossible to prescribe a single catechesis for this sacrament."[55] Many programs are including elements of social justice and community service. Catechists consider that the correct approach can be a real problem. One catechist puts it this way: "Catechists who are asked to prepare children of grade school age for Confirmation are presently given an unenviable task. On what theology of Confirmation are they to base their catechesis?"[56] In any case, the entire parish community must be involved as well as the parents, the sponsors, the catechists, and the clergy.

The liturgical service of the sacrament should reflect a communal dimension. The diverse functions played by different parishioners in adult initiation with their corresponding liturgical expressions should serve as a model for the confirmation service. "Attention should be paid to the festive and solemn character of the liturgical service, especially its significance for the local church" [4]. The service should convey that the local church is a Spirit-filled community and that the confirmands are being made part of that in a very special way on this occasion. The presence of the bishop in their midst would serve to broaden their vision to include the entire diocesan church, and indeed the entire church universal.

UNITY OF THE SACRAMENTS OF INITIATION
The *Rite of Confirmation,* like the *Rite of Baptism for Children* and the *Rite of Christian Initiation of Adults,*

clearly underscores that there are three sacraments of initiation—baptism, confirmation, and eucharist—and that they complement one another in that order. When confirmation is conferred on those who have already been baptized, renewal of baptismal promises is made. This renewal of promises takes place after the homily and immediately before the laying on of hands and the anointing with chrism. This renewal connotes two things. First, it shows the intimate connection between the two sacraments of baptism and confirmation. Second, it shows that confirmation is not the same thing as the ratification of a previous baptism. If that were all that confirmation connoted, the new rite would be guilty of proposing a duplication. One of the guiding principles of the Vatican II liturgical reform is the elimination of useless repetitions.[57] Thus, the very inclusion of the renewal of previous baptismal promises precludes confirmation as simply a mature reaffirmation of a previous baptism. The reality celebrated by the anointing with chrism, which is done by the hand-laying and prayer, must be something more.

Also, the new rite underscores confirmation's connection with the eucharist. Thomas Aquinas stated an important principle: "The eucharist is the summit of the spiritual life, and the goal of all the sacraments."[58] Paul VI in his Apostolic Constitution, *Divinae Consortium Naturae*, said: "Confirmation is so closely linked with the holy eucharist that the faithful, after being signed by holy baptism and confirmation, are incorporated fully into the body of Christ by participation in the eucharist."[59] The *Rite of Confirmation* takes this principle seriously: "Ordinarily confirmation takes place within Mass in order to express more clearly the fundamental connection of this sacrament with the entirety of Christian initiation. The latter reaches its culmination in the communion of the body and blood of Christ. The newly confirmed should therefore participate in the eucharist which completes their Christian initiation"

[13]. Then it takes up a special case: "If the candidates for confirmation are children who have not received the eucharist and are not admitted to their first communion at this liturgical celebration or if there are other special circumstances, confirmation should be celebrated outside Mass. When this occurs, there should first be a celebration of the word of God" [13]. In other words, in such a case, the anomaly of such children not completing their initiation by receiving communion during that eucharist would be too manifest. Better not to have a eucharist celebrated!

In conclusion, it may be said that the new *Rite of Confirmation* makes a valiant attempt to restore the intrinsic connection between the three sacraments of initiation. It recommends that "adult catechumens and children who are baptized at an age when they are old enough for catechesis should ordinarily be admitted to confirmation and the eucharist at the same time they receive baptism" [11]. When this is done, confirmation replaces the first postbaptismal anointing. Unfortunately, however, delaying the confirmation of young children until after first eucharist (a possibility given in [11]) provides the potential for undoing that valiant attempt to restore the unity of the three sacraments of initiation.

NOTES

1. *Ordo Confirmationis* (Typis Polyglottis Vaticanis, Vatican City 1971). English: *Rite of Confirmation* (National Conference of Catholic Bishops: Bishops' Committee on the Liturgy, Washington, D.C. 1975). See *The Rites of the Catholic Church* (Pueblo, New York 1976), pp. 287–334. The English translation of the rite was approved "provisionally" by the Congregation for Divine Worship on December 16, 1971 and "finally" on May 5, 1975. The effective date (mandatory usage) of the finally approved text for the United States was September 15, 1977. Except for the Apostolic Constitution, paragraph

numbers of the rite will not be footnoted, but will be bracketed in the text itself.

2. *Rite of Baptism for Children* (United States Catholic Conference, Washington, D.C. 1969). See *The Rites*, pp. 183–283. The General Introduction to all three sacraments of initiation was issued with this document; see *The Rites*, pp. 3–11.

3. *Rite of Christian Initiation of Adults* (United States Catholic Conference, Washington, D.C. 1974). See *The Rites*, pp. 13–181)

4. Aidan Kavanagh, *The Shape of Baptism: The Rite of Christian Initiation* (Pueblo, New York 1978), pp. 126–127.

5. *Constitution on the Sacred Liturgy*, no. 71. See *Documents on the Liturgy 1963–1979* (Liturgical Press, Collegeville, Minn. 1982), no. 71.

6. *The Rites*, p. 290.

7. Ibid., pp. 290–291.

8. On this whole issue see Gerard Austin, "The Essential Rite of Confirmation and Liturgical Tradition," *Ephemerides Liturgicae* 86 (1972), pp. 214–224; also, "What Has Happened to Confirmation?" *Worship* 50 (1976), pp. 420–426.

9. See Damien Van den Eynde, "The Theory of the Composition of the Sacraments in Early Scholasticism," *Franciscan Studies* 12 (1952), p. 20.

10. *The Rites*, p. 294.

11. Ibid., p. 295.

12. See Louis Ligier, *La confirmation: sens et conjoncture oecuménique hier et aujourd'hui* (Beauchesne, Paris 1973). The author makes a strong case for the primacy of the imposition of hands over the anointing, not just for the West but for the East as well.

13. *The Rites*, p. 296.

14. See Pietro Gasparri, *Codicis Iuris Canonici Fontes*, vol. IV (Typis Polyglottis Vaticanis, Rome 1926), pp. 326–327.

15. Canon 780, 1.

16. J. A. Abbo and J. D. Hannan, *The Sacred Canons* (Herder, St. Louis and London 1952), vol. 1, p. 777.

17. *The Rites*, p. 296. The 1983 Code of Canon Law repeats this wording in its Canon 880.

18. This particular pontifical is nowhere to be found today, but we know of the confirmation rubric due to the comments of Joseph Catalani. See Joseph Catalani, *Pontificale in tres partes distributum Clementis VIII ac Urbani VIII*, vol. 1 (Paris 1850), p. 5.

19. Dom Bernard Botte was the head of the commission that worked on the preliminary draft of the new rite of confirmation. In his memoirs he states that the suppression of the rubric of the imposition of the hand simultaneous with the anointing was not an accidental omission, but an intentional suppression of a gesture which he considered "peu naturel et tout à fait inexpressif." Bernard Botte, *Le mouvement liturgique: témoignage et souvenirs* (Desclée, Paris 1973), p. 196.

20. *Acta Apostolicae Sedis* 64 (1972), p. 526; also may be found in *Notitiae* 8 (1972), p. 281. See *Documents on the Liturgy*, no. 2529.

21. "Chrismatio ita peracta manus impositionem sufficienter manifestat."

22. For a general survey of the role of the laying on of hands in all the sacraments, see Godfrey Diekmann, "The Laying on of Hands: The Basic Sacramental Rite," *Proceedings of the Catholic Theological Society of America* 29 (1974), pp. 339–351.

23. The previous formula, "I sign you with the sign of the cross and confirm you with the chrism of salvation, in the name of the Father and of the Son and of the Holy Spirit," had come from the twelfth century. See Michel Andrieu, *Le Pontifical Romain du XIIe Siècle* (Biblioteca Apostolica Vaticana, Vatican City 1938), p. 247.

24. On October 25, 1973, Pope Paul VI reserved to himself the power to approve directly all the translations of the sacramental forms into the vernacular. See Congregation for Divine Worship, Circular Letter of the Secretary of State on Norms for Translating Liturgical Books: *AAS* 66 (1974), pp. 98–99; *Documents on the Liturgy*, nos. 904–908.

25. Sacred Congregation for Divine Worship, Letter to presidents of the English-speaking conferences of bishops, on papal approval of the translation of the sacramental form of Confirmation, 5 May 1975. See *Newsletter: Bishops' Committee on the Liturgy* 11 (1975), pp. 25–26; *Documents on the Liturgy*, no. 910.

26. His proposed wording was slightly different: "Accipe signaculum Spiritus Sancti qui tibi datur." See Botte, *Le mouvement*, p. 196.

27. See Louis Ligier, *La confirmation*, pp. 208–209.

28. *The Rites*, p. 291.

29. Ibid.

30. Ibid., p. 292.

31. As was said in chapter 1, not even the so-called "Riddle of Samaria" problem of Acts 8:17 would give such a proof due to the complexity of the issue.

32. See Burkhard Neunheuser, *Baptism and Confirmation* (Herder and Herder, New York 1964), p. 52.

33. See *Dogmatic Constitution on the Church*, nos. 26–27; Flannery, pp. 381–383. For a brief overview, see Antonio Mostaza Rodriguez, "The Minister of Confirmation" in N. Edelby, T. Jiménez-Urresti, and P. Huizing (eds.), *The Sacraments in Theology and Canon Law* (Paulist Press, New York 1968), pp. 28–36.

34. See P. M. Gy, "Histoire liturgique du sacrement de confirmation," *La Maison-Dieu* 58 (1959), p. 144. It is interesting to note that while the use of Latin in the confirmation ceremony prohibited an understanding on the part of the people, no such risk was to be allowed when it came to a question of authority!

35. *The Rites*, p. 292.

36. *AAS* 72 (1980), p. 105. The response was in the affirmative, however, for those Catholics who had joined other religions and who were coming into full communion. See also *AAS* 67 (1975) 348.

37. See Botte, p. 197.

38. Since 1974 in the Archdiocese of Brisbane, Australia, confirmation is administered in most parishes on Pentecost Sunday by the parochial pastor. The bishops also confirm on other occasions.

39. Canon 782, 1.

40. Session VII, Canon 3; Denzinger, no. 1630.

41. *Orientalium Ecclesiarum* no. 13; Flannery, pp. 445–446.

42. *Lumen Gentium* no. 26; Flannery, p. 382.

43. See *Acta pontificae commissionum centralis praeparationae concilii oecumenici vaticani II* 2 (Typis Polyglottis Vaticanis, Vatican City 1962), pp. 105–107.

44. It should be noted, however, that the terminology of the *Rite of Confirmation* is not totally consistent; paragraph eight speaks of the "extraordinary minister," as does the title of Chapter Three.

45. Canon 882.

46. See Bernard Botte, "A propos de la confirmation," *Nouvelle Revue Théologique* 88 (1966), p. 848.

47. See Pietro Gasparri, *Codicis Iuris Canonici Fontes*, vol. III (Typis Polyglottis Vaticanis, Vatican City 1925), pp. 515–516.

48. Canon 788.

49. *AAS* 24 (1932), pp. 271–272.

50. Ibid., 44 (1952), p. 496.

51. *Newsletter, Bishops' Committee on the Liturgy* 8 (1972) nos. 5–6.

52. See Botte, "A propos de la confirmation," p. 852.

53. Canon 891: "The sacrament of confirmation is to be conferred on the faithful at about the age of discretion unless the conference of bishops determines another age or there is danger of death or in the judgment of the minister a grave cause urges otherwise" (translations are taken from *Code of Canon Law*, Canon Law Society of America, Washington, D.C. 1983). For a very thorough study of the new canons on confirmation see Michael James Balhoff, "The Legal Interrelatedness of the Sacraments of Initiation: New Canonical Developments in the Latin Rite from Vatican II to the 1983 Code of Canon Law" (unpublished doctoral dissertation, the Catholic University of America 1984).

54. Cyrille Vogel (ed.), *Le Pontifical Romano-Germanique du dixième siècle*, vol. 2 (Studi e Testi 227) (Biblioteca Apostolica Vaticana, Vatican City 1963), p. 109.

55. *Sharing the Light of Faith: National Catechetical Directory for Catholics of the United States* (U.S. Catholic Conference, Washington, D.C. 1979), para. 119.

56. Anne Marie Mongoven, *Signs of Catechesis* (Paulist Press, New York 1979), p. 46.

57. See *Constitution on the Sacred Liturgy* no. 34 (*Documents on the Liturgy,* no. 34).

58. *Summa Theologiae* III, q. 73, art. 3.

59. *The Rites,* p. 292.

Chapter Three

The New Rite of Confirmation
in the Episcopal Church

In recent years almost every area of Christian theological investigation has profited from ecumenical cooperation. Protestant, Orthodox, and Catholic theologians have shared their traditions with one another, resulting in a deeper understanding for all involved. This understanding is particularly true in the area of Christian initiation, since different traditions have emphasized or guarded over the centuries one or more of the particular aspects of the economy of the initiation sacraments. For deeper insights into the meaning of that step of initiation called confirmation, Roman Catholics can profit from looking to the Anglican tradition, and in particular, to the interesting developments of this century that have been taking place in the Episcopal Church in the United States.[1]

In the Anglican tradition the term "confirmation" has always carried a dual meaning: on the one hand, it connotes a sacramental, postbaptismal rite; while on the other hand, it bespeaks a catechetical rite, the reaffirmation of one's previous baptismal promises. This problem of terminology—or perhaps better, richness of terminology—can be traced back to the very beginning, to the baptism and confirmation rites in the *Book of Common Prayer* of 1549 and 1552.[2]

PRAYER BOOK OF 1549
In the Prayer Book of 1549 Archbishop Cranmer, chief architect of the book, accomplished radical initiatory

65

reforms. Under the influence of the continental reformers he strove to create one single rite of Christian initiation. The postbaptismal chrismation follows the giving of the white vesture immediately after the water-bath. The rite says: "The priest shall anoint the infant upon the head, saying: 'Almighty God, the Father of our Lord Jesus Christ, who hath regenerated thee by water and the Holy Ghost, and hath given unto thee remission of all thy sins, he vouchsafe to anoint thee with the unction of his Holy Spirit, and bring thee to the inheritance of everlasting life. Amen.' "[3] J. D. C. Fisher thinks that the words "the unction of his Holy Spirit" here could be interpreted as giving this unction the force of a presbyteral confirmation.[4] Certainly there is ambiguity here as to just what Cranmer intended, and it is probably better not to refer to the anointing as "presbyteral confirmation" as Fisher does, since Cranmer will reserve the term confirmation for the later episcopal rite of reaffirmation of one's baptism.

Nevertheless, Marion Hatchett points out that Cranmer's wording of the chrismation prayer shows he intended to perpetuate some ideas of the medieval rite of confirmation at this point in the baptismal ritual.[5] The original phrase of the Sarum rite, following the *Gelasianum*, which accompanied the first of the postbaptismal anointings had read, "anoint thee with the chrism of salvation." Cranmer substituted: "anoint thee with the unction of his Holy Spirit." Hatchett comments, "The original behind the substitution must be 'unctio spiritus sancti', which was a common phrase among theologians of the Middle Ages, but it was applied by them to that unique second post-baptismal anointing normally performed by a bishop which was a peculiarity of the Roman rite."[6] This view would argue that Cranmer seems to have drawn some of the ideas of medieval confirmation into the context of and immediately juxtaposed with the water-rite. The manner in which he did so, however, indicates a certain theological ambivalence rather than a clearly thought through retention of the medieval theology of confirmation, and attributes to Cranmer a greater concern for medieval confirmation than he actually had.

Nevertheless Hatchett remarks, "Having provided in a sense for the rite called 'confirmation' in the Middle Ages to be incorporated into the baptismal rite, the 1549 Prayer Book then provided a rite entitled 'confirmation' which followed the precedents of the Bohemian Brethren."[7] In this he parted with Calvin and Zwingli, who had abandoned the rite in their churches. He entitled the rite "Confirmation, wherein is contained a catechism for children." The rite is performed by the bishop for children who are able to say the articles of their faith, the Lord's prayer, the ten commandments, and to answer the other questions contained in the catechism. The ceremony opens with the bishop saying the prayer for the gifts of the Holy Spirit from the Sarum Manual, which in turn derived from the sixth-century Gelasian Sacramentary.[8] "Then the bishop shall cross them in the forehead, and lay his hands upon their heads, saying: N., I sign thee with the sign of the cross, and lay my hand upon thee, in the name of the Father and of the Son and of the Holy Ghost. Amen."[9] Unlike the practice of the Sarum Manual, there is no chrism used here.

The last rubric of the rite is important: "And there shall none be admitted to the holy communion, until such time as he be confirmed."[10] This stipulation, known as the "Confirmation rubric," governed liturgical practice until quite recently. Hatchett comments that the rite of confirmation "was to be administered when the child approaches the age of culpability, for a benefit of the rite is the receiving of 'strength and defense' against the temptations of the world, the flesh, and the devil which are associated with that period in a child's life."[11]

We see, then, the origins of the duality of meaning of the term "confirmation" in the Anglican tradition: it is both a sacramental rite attached to the water-bath and a later owning of a previous baptism. The latter meaning reflects an understanding of confirmation that grew in acceptance during the sixteenth century.

PRAYER BOOK OF 1552

Between the 1549 Prayer Book and that of 1552 Martin Bucer wrote *Censura*, his critique of the 1549 Prayer Book.[12] Bucer's criticisms were based on principles of (1) eliminating ceremonial actions, especially those involving such material things as oil, which did not have clear warrant in scripture, and (2) eliminating duplications, such as introducing in prayers and actions at the church door themes that would shortly be repeated in the central actions at the font. Bucer's work influenced the 1552 rite—for example, in abolishing the vesting in a white robe and the anointing with chrism, both of which, in the 1549 rite, followed the water-bath. After the water-bath of the 1552 rite:

"the priest shall make a cross upon the child's forehead, saying: 'We receive this child into the congregation of Christ's flock, and do sign him with the sign of the cross, in token that hereafter he shall not be ashamed to confess the faith of Christ crucified, and manfully to fight under his banner against sin, the world and the devil, and to continue Christ's faithful soldier and servant unto his life's end. Amen.' "[13]

In the 1549 rite this prayer and consignation had formed part of the service at the church door, but as Fisher explains, "when in 1552 the service at the church door was abolished, this consignation was removed from among the introductory prayers, and

68

placed immediately after the baptism itself in such close juxtaposition that it has become possible for the ignorant to mistake it for the essential act of baptism."[14] Some authors argue that it is easily understood from the content of this prayer that it carried some of the weight of the medieval rite called confirmation, giving one the strength to confess and defend the faith. Yet it is interesting to note that this rite was not to be supplied in the case of an infant who had been baptized privately and who was later being received publicly, which certainly would caution one from equating the prayer completely with medieval confirmation. Hatchett comments that since the prayer was not to be later supplied, it was "quite clear that such a ceremony is not essential for the completion of baptism but constitutes an explanation of what has happened in the baptism."[15]

The 1552 rite of confirmation by a bishop places greater stress on the recipient's ability to recite the catechism: "And there shall none be admitted to the Holy Communion, until such time as he can say the catechism and be confirmed."[16] Instead of the teaching of the catechism being mandated one Sunday in six as in the 1549 rite, now "the curate of every parish, or some other at his appointment, shall diligently upon Sundays and holy days half an hour before Evensong, openly in the church instruct and examine so many children of his parish sent unto him as the time will serve, and as he shall think convenient, in some part of this catechism."[17] Thus, confirmation was closely connected with catechesis and with personal accountability in matters of faith.

In the confirmation rite of the Prayer Book of 1552 the signing of the forehead was discontinued, and a number of changes were made in the prayers. The prayer before the hand-laying inserts the "strengthening" concept. The words accompanying the hand-laying become: "Defend, O Lord, this child with thy heavenly grace, that he may continue thine for ever, and daily increase in the Holy Spirit more and more, until he come unto thy everlasting kingdom. Amen."[18] Most important, the 1549 prayer, "Sign them, O Lord, " with the crucial phrase, "strength [sic] them with the inward unction of the Holy Ghost," was omitted.

So it was, then, that the confused Western inheritance of the initiatory rite and teaching was addressed by the Anglican Reformation in the sixteenth century. Cranmer left no rationale for his work, yet it is possible to argue that even though he lacked much of the material available today for understanding the early history of initiatory practice, he sought to restore the lost unity of the baptismal liturgy. That he did this, as some authors recently argue, by incorporating into the baptismal rite elements of medieval confirmation seems difficult to prove. Indeed, if he did, his intent was not so perceived until the present century. Cranmer was not taken up with confirmation. For him the Holy Spirit was given in baptism; he was interested in confirmation as a catechetical phenomenon. Thus he retained an episcopal rite of confirmation signifying the coming of age in the life of faith. There is enough unclarity in the sixteenth-century Prayer Books that Anglicans have gone on debating initiatory issues down through the centuries. Unfortunately they have usually fastened on confirmation rather than on baptism, where Cranmer's work was more creative.

It is interesting to note that an explicit ratification of the promises of baptism did not appear in the Prayer Book confirmation rite until the revision of 1662, even though this public ratification was thought to be a principal function of the occasion. Only after a century of the existence of the Prayer Book rites did the bishops begin asking the confirmands: "Do ye here, in the presence of God, and of this Congregation renew the solemn promise and vow that was made in your name at your Baptism; ratifying and confirming the same in your own persons, and acknowledging yourselves bound to believe and to do all those things, which your Godfathers and Godmothers then undertook for you?"[19]

The complexity in the Western tradition of initiatory rites, reflected by the variety in the early Prayer Books, gave rise to 400 years of divided opinion among Anglicans as to the meaning of confirmation. The confirmation itself, according to the Prayer Books of 1552, 1662, and the worldwide Anglican diaspora, was an episcopal ministration, following a period of catechesis. Further, communicant status was contingent on confirmation, a rubric that goes all the way back to 1285, having been put into force by John Peckham, Archbishop of Canterbury.[20] Only since the nineteenth century has the rite been administered in a methodical, pastorally effective way at episcopal visitations, so regularly that it could be expected that most Episcopalians would have the opportunity to be confirmed.

This rather consistent Prayer Book rite has been interpreted in different contexts. As Louis Weil puts it, "Confirmation, as the medieval Church came to know it, and as it was in turn modified within the Anglican tradition, is now seen as a constantly evolving practice which reflected the Church's adaptation to changed situations."[21] Some Anglican scholars maintained that confirmation is a sacramental rite with a biblical basis, imparting in some sense the Holy Spirit and necessary to full standing in Christian life and community. Although not calling confirmation directly a sacrament, the great writer of the seventeenth century, Jeremy Taylor, refers to it as a "Holy Rite." He summarizes the benefits of the rite: "(1) But the principal thing is this: confirmation is the consummation and perfection, the corroboration and strength, of baptism and baptismal grace: for in baptism we undertake to do our duty, but in confirmation we receive strength to do it. . . . (2) In confirmation we receive the Holy Ghost as the earnest of our inheritance, as the seal of our salvation."[22] Other Anglicans saw confirmation as an addition to the baptismal rite made in very early centuries, but one that does not add anything essential. This portion of the baptismal rite, having become detached in the West, now provides a valuable moment that speaks of the additional strength of the Holy Spirit required as a Christian moves from the relative dependence of childhood to the relative self-dependence of adulthood. Some, drawing on sources from the early church, stressed the sacramental side of confirmation; it is God's gift to us. Others, drawing on developmental studies and social factors, stressed the catechetical side; confirmation is our response to God.[23]

MODERN REFORMS

This internal Anglican debate became vigorous in the late nineteenth and early twentieth centuries, with scholarly arguments on both sides. Anglican liturgists appealed to the early church, and it was startling when important historical discoveries made clear the difference between initiatory practices of the early centuries and those of the modern church and the Prayer Book. All the disputants had to accept the norm of the traditional Prayer Book rites. Changes might be desired, but it seemed unlikely that fundamental modifications could readily be agreed on.

But under the influence of the ecumenical liturgical movement a thorough, systematic reconsideration of liturgy has been undertaken in Anglican churches in the mid-twentieth century. The theological restlessness over confirmation needed to be addressed. It was not certain at first whether liturgical rite, theological understanding, and pastoral practice could grow toward greater coherence. Starting in the 1950s, the Standing Liturgical Commission of the Episcopal Church in the United States reviewed the rites of Christian initiation.

By the early 1970s, it seemed valuable to disentangle the two strands of meaning that had become mingled in the prayer book rite of confirmation. These meanings grew from different historical contexts and, in the modern situation, tended in different directions. Daniel Stevick, a member of the Drafting Committee on Christian Initiation for the *Proposed Book of Common Prayer* of 1977, puts the matter in focus by making a distinction:

"Two principal themes and sources are distinguishable: (1) One line of ancestry of Confirmation is the post-baptismal blessing, which traces to the early Church. This rite took many forms, but in the early Church, it was always continuous with Baptism itself. But by the later Middle Ages in the West, it had become part of a second stage of initiation. (2) Another line of ancestry came from the Reformation. It is the ratification of baptismal promises. This function had no ritual continuity with the early Church. Of course, the early Christians did teach candidates before Baptism, and persons being baptized professed their faith. But the transfer of these features of initiation to Confirmation, as a second and later stage of initiation, has commended itself in many of the churches of the modern West as a way of dealing with what had come to be felt as the psychological incompleteness of infant Baptism. One rite was sacramental, the other catechetical. One derived from the liturgy of becoming a Christian; the other was something done by a Christian at a certain stage of his maturation. One signified the Holy Spirit, the other the renewal of promises made at an earlier rite in one's behalf. One emphasized what God does, the other what man does."[24]

73

Thus the committee attempted to separate and to give a different treatment to two aspects of confirmation: (1) the sacramental seal and (2) the ratification of the baptismal promises. Some members wanted to drop the term "confirmation" completely, feeling that it is not an early or universal term, but one that has been clouded by ambiguities. But in the final Prayer Book text, the resolution (heavily influenced by the House of Bishops) was to reserve the term for the latter of the two aspects.[25]

The first aspect, the sacramental seal, is found with the water-bath. Immediately after the baptism with water and the trinitarian name, there is a prayer that begins as thanksgiving but turns to a petition for the gifts of the Spirit for the newly baptized. This prayer is a reworked version of the one that formerly stood in the confirmation rite. Following this prayer, "The Bishop or Priest places a hand on the person's head, marking on the forehead the sign of the cross (using Chrism if desired) and saying to each one, 'N., you are sealed by the Holy Spirit in Baptism and marked as Christ's own for ever. Amen.' "[26] The prayer is led and the seal administered by a priest except when a bishop is present. Thus this aspect of confirmation is now a presbyteral rite except in those cases when a bishop is taking part in the baptismal liturgy. The juxtaposition of these two sacramental actions as moments within the rite of baptism is an attempt, using the materials of the Anglican tradition, to articulate explicitly the unity of the baptismal liturgy.

The second aspect, the ratification of baptismal promises, is handled differently. In the Prayer Book baptismal liturgy, members of the congregation (along with the persons newly baptized or sponsors who speak for them) affirm the creed and some important associated promises. Thus for those already baptized, each baptism is routinely an occasion of renewing one's own baptismal covenant.[27] But for any Christian, this renewal of the gift, promises, and pledges of baptism may be a powerful way of expressing important moments in one's own life in relation to Christ and the church. When a bishop presides at the initiatory liturgy, after the baptisms, the sacramental sealing, and an expression of welcome, the newly baptized persons and their sponsors retire, and those persons for whom special significance attaches to the congregational act of reaffirmation that has just been made step forward with sponsors. The bishop prays for these persons as a group. In working out the liturgical vocabulary of the revised Prayer Book, the term "confirmation" was (not to everyone's satisfaction) reserved for the occasion when persons baptized at an early age "make a mature public affirmation of their faith and commitment to the responsibilities of their Baptism and receive the laying on of hands by the bishop."[28] The bishop lays hands on and prays for each of these persons. The same occasion is used for the reception of persons who were baptized in another Christian communion but now intend to live out the commitments of that baptism in the fellowship of the Episcopal Church, and it is used for persons who for individual reasons are making an act of recommitment. In reception and reaffirmation, unlike confirmation, no episcopal laying on of hands is specified.[29] Thus the second aspect of confirmation is retained in the Episcopal Church's new rite, and somewhat extended. No sacramental right or privilege depends on it. It is not meant to shape some sort of elite within the baptized. It is not an act done once in childhood or adolescence and never done again, for the heart of the action—the searching renewal of the fundamental covenant of grace and faith—may be appropriate at later crises or intense moments of life in the Spirit. The *first* occasion of such a renewal for a person baptized as an infant is "confirmation." But the repeatable rite of "reaffirmation" allows for the ritualization of moments of passage in Christian experience over a lifetime.

CONCLUSION

To a Roman Catholic viewing these revised rites it appears that the rite of initiation has been reunited after its millennium-long fragmentation; the sacraments of baptism and confirmation (in the Roman Catholic view) have been joined just as baptism and chrismation have always been joined in Eastern Orthodox liturgies. Yet for the Roman Catholic theologian the phrase, "in Baptism," in the sealing formula ("N., you are sealed by the Holy Spirit in Baptism and marked as Christ's own for ever. Amen.") might cause difficulty by implying that this act of sealing is not a distinct sacramental rite, separate from the water-bath itself. The Episcopalian sacramental theologian would counter that the term "Baptism" here refers to the totality of the rite including all its subsidiary ceremonies. Still, it is interesting to note that hesitancy over the phrase "in Baptism" of the sealing formula is shared by people who had a part in drafting the new rite and that the final wording represents a compromise that was only grudgingly accepted.[30]

The new rite is silent as to the "Confirmation rubric." In 1970, the General Convention of Houston, Texas, had authorized "that children be admitted to Holy Communion before Confirmation, subject to the direction and guidance of the Ordinary."[31] In some Episcopalian circles the communicating of infants and young children has begun.[32] One hopes that this will cause others, including those who are members of other churches, to reexamine the whole question. The new rite implies that the fundamental right to eucharist comes from baptism and not from an extrinsic factor such as the "age of discretion." Any argument against communicating infants could equally argue against in-

76

fant baptism. Just as in a natural family infants are fed lovingly right from the beginning, so in the church this care should be carried out through the entire process of growth, with the child moving progressively into a deeper and deeper understanding of just what is taking place when it is fed at the Lord's Table.

The new initiation rite of the 1979 *Book of Common Prayer* of the Episcopal Church has done a great service by facing many of the problems and issues involved in the economy of Christian initiation. It will require a number of years for the rite to become widely used and understood by Episcopalians, and in turn to be discussed by other Christian churches. Perhaps the rite's greatest contribution for Roman Catholics will be to help them separate in their own thinking the two aspects of confirmation: the sacramental sealing and the ratification of previous baptismal promises. Episcopalian Bishop Frederick Wolf of Maine, a member of the committee drafting the new rites, explains that certain basic considerations were reflected in the process of the revision of the initiation rites:

"First, the new rites are shaped by the conviction that Baptism bestows full membership in the Church and therefore fully bestows the sevenfold gifts of the Holy Spirit. Secondly, Confirmation rites are shaped by the conviction that Confirmation is the mature, freely determined renewal of our baptismal vows and the personal appropriation of the gifts bestowed in Baptism, with the recognition that Confirmation is one great moment in a series of lifelong moments of deepening commitment and of appropriation of the baptismal gifts."[33]

At what age should that "great moment" take place? There is no set age. Many Episcopalians see it not as something for an adolescent to do in going through a "puberty rite," but rather as a rite of personal commitment for an adult.[34]

The Episcopalian solution has many advantages. It disentangles things that for too long have been confused. Confirmation is seen under both aspects: (1) a postbaptismal sealing[35], and (2) a mature reaffirmation of a previous baptism. Episcopalians have retained liturgically the term confirmation only for the latter while maintaining the baptismal sealing in its rightful position. The Roman Catholic reform has restored the seal to baptism and united the two postbaptismal anointings into one in the case of adults and older children. The problem still remains, however, for those baptized as infants. For infants, except in the case of danger of death, baptism is deprived of its seal. Confirmation is then made into something it was never meant to be. The need for a ratification in adulthood of one's infant baptism is an important thing, but it must never be the cause of robbing baptism of its traditional complement: the sacrament of confirmation, the sealing of the Spirit leading to its fulfillment in the Table of the Lord.

NOTES

1. I am greatly indebted to Professor Daniel B. Stevick (Episcopal Divinity School, Boston, Mass.) for the help he gave me with this chapter. For the genesis of the new initiation rite of the Episcopal Church in the United States see his "The Liturgics of Confirmation" in Kendig B. Cully (ed.), *Confirmation Re-examined* (Morehouse-Barlow, Wilton, Conn. 1982), pp. 61–79. For the total contemporary Anglican picture, see David R. Holeton, "Christian Initiation in Some Anglican Provinces," *Studia Liturgica* 12 (1977), pp. 129–150. He considers work that has been going on in the various provinces outside the Church of England; for an account of the work within the English church itself see Ronald C. D. Jasper, "Christian Initiation: The Anglican Position," *Studia Liturgica* 12 (1977), pp. 116–125.

2. For an excellent survey of the history of confirmation in the Anglican Church see Frank C. Quinn, "Contemporary Liturgical Revision: The Revised Rites of Confirmation in the

Roman Catholic Church and in the American Episcopal Church," unpublished doctoral dissertation, University of Notre Dame 1978, pp. 277–395.

3. J. D. C. Fisher, *Christian Initiation: The Reformation Period* (SPCK, London 1970), p. 94.

4. Ibid., note 5.

5. See Marion Hatchett, "The Rite of 'Confirmation' in the Book of Common Prayer and in Authorized Services 1973," *Anglican Theological Review* 56 (1974), p. 300.

6. Ibid.

7. Ibid., p. 301.

8. *Liber Sacramentorum Romanae Aeclesiae Ordinis Anni Circuli,* L. C. Mohlberg (ed.) (Casa Editrice Herder, Rome 1960), no. 451.

9. Fisher, p. 242. It is interesting to note that the next rubric, referring back to the action described here, uses not the plural "hands," but the traditional "hand."

10. Ibid., p. 243.

11. Hatchett, p. 301.

12. May be found in Fisher, pp. 96–105, 244–250.

13. Fisher, pp. 110.

14. Ibid., note 2.

15. Hatchett, p. 306.

16. Fisher, p. 252.

17. Ibid.

18. Ibid., p. 251.

19. Peter J. Jagger, *Christian Initiation: 1552–1969* (SPCK, London 1970), p. 30.

20. See Urban T. Holmes, *Confirmation: The Celebration of Maturity in Christ* (Seabury, New York 1975), pp. 43–44.

21. Louis Weil, *Sacraments and Liturgy: The Outward Signs* (Blackwell, Oxford 1983), p. 76.

22. As quoted in Harry Boone Porter, *Jeremy Taylor, Liturgist* (SPCK, London 1979), p. 35.

23. See Charles P. Price and Louis Weil, *Liturgy for Living* (Seabury, New York 1979), pp. 97–131.

24. Daniel B. Stevick, *Holy Baptism Together With a Form for the Affirmation of Baptismal Vows With the Laying-on of Hands by the Bishop Also Called Confirmation,* Supplement to Prayer Book Studies 26 (Church Hymnal Corporation, New York 1973), pp. 49–50.

25. *Proposed: The Book of Common Prayer* (Seabury, New York 1977), p. 309. The rite is the same in the approved 1979 *The Book of Common Prayer,* and the pagination is identical. The term "confirmation" was reserved only for a believer's first ratification of the baptismal promises that were made by one's godparents on one's behalf in infancy and not used for reception (one who was baptized in another fellowship who wishes to become a member of the Episcopal Church) or reaffirmation (when a person whose practice of the Christian life has become perfunctory or has completely lapsed awakes again to the call of Christ and desires to show his or her response publicly and receive a strengthening gift of the Spirit for renewal). The intervening rite, the one authorized by the General Convention of 1973, *Holy Baptism,* Prayer Book Studies 26 (Seabury, New York 1973), had used the term confirmation for all three cases, causing a good deal of confusion.

26. Ibid., p. 308.

27. Ibid., pp. 304 f. The same material is repeated on pp. 416 f. for those occasions when "renewal" is made without an actual baptism.

28. Ibid., p. 412.

29. Ibid. In practice, bishops adapt their words and gestures to the persons and the situations present, guided by good pastoral sense.

30. The formula of the initial draft seems to have been a better one: "N., you are sealed by the Holy Spirit and marked as Christ's own for ever." The formula of the new Lutheran rite is "N., child of God, you have been sealed by the Holy

Spirit and marked with the cross of Christ forever." *Lutheran Book of Worship* (Augsburg, Minneapolis 1978), p. 124.

31. *Services for Trial Use* (Church Hymnal Corporation, New York 1971), p. 21.

32. For compelling reasons in favor of the practice, see Price and Weil, pp. 130–131.

33. Frederick B. Wolf, "Christian Initiation" in H. Barry Evans (ed.), *Prayer Book Renewal* (Seabury, New York 1978), pp. 39–40.

34. See Leonel L. Mitchell, "The Theology of Christian Initiation and the Proposed Book of Common Prayer," *Anglican Theological Review* 60 (1978), p. 416.

35. Marion Hatchett says: "The baptismal rite of the present edition maintains the traditional Prayer Book pattern of baptism with water, followed by a signation which represents the 'confirmation' of the Roman rite." *Commentary on the American Prayer Book* (Seabury, New York 1980), p. 267.

Chapter Four

Confirmation in Protestant Churches

The rites of initiation of the Episcopal Church in the United States have been singled out because of their interesting evolution and development. As the reform in the Episcopal Church was reaching its final culmination under the supervision of the various General Conventions, other Christians as well as Episcopalians were greatly aided by explanations of the new rites found in the "Prayer Book Studies" series. The widespread appreciation of these studies underscored the need for catechesis to accompany any change in liturgical practices and texts.

STATEMENTS OF THE WORLD COUNCIL OF CHURCHES

A similar contribution was made on the worldwide level by statements issued by the World Council of Churches through its Faith and Order Commission. The World Council has subjected the question of Christian initiation to ecumenical debate for the past fifty years. The results can be seen particularly in two important Faith and Order Papers: *One Baptism, One Eucharist and a Mutually Recognized Ministry* in 1975 and *Baptism, Eucharist and Ministry* in 1982.[1] The latter is often referred to as the Lima text as it was the product of a conference of over one hundred theologians meeting in Lima, Peru. They came from all parts of the world and represented virtually all the major church traditions: Eastern Orthodox, Oriental Orthodox, Roman Catholic,

Old Catholic, Lutheran, Anglican, Reformed, Methodist, United, Disciples, Baptist, Adventist, and Pentecostal. Their vote on acceptance of the statement was unanimous.

Both statements recognize the central position in the church's life that baptism and eucharist hold. The central meaning of baptism itself is participation in the death and resurrection of Christ. The Lima text does not stress as forcefully the centrality of Jesus' baptism by John as does the earlier statement that reads, "The baptism with which Jesus himself was baptized (Mark 10:38) provides the key to common understanding."[2] The Lima text, on the other hand, brings out in a better way the ethical implications of initiation: "Those baptized are given as part of their baptismal experience a new ethical orientation under the guidance of the Holy Spirit."[3] "They [Christians] acknowledge that baptism, as a baptism into Christ's death, has ethical implications which not only call for personal sanctification, but also motivate Christians to strive for the realization of the will of God in all realms of life (Rom. 6:9 ff; Gal. 3: 27–28; I Peter 2:21–4:6)."[4] Baptism is seen as creating the bond of unity among Christians: "Through their one baptism, Christians are brought into union with Christ and with each other and into the life of the Church Universal as well as the community of the local church. . . ."[5] "Therefore, our one baptism into Christ constitutes a call to the churches to overcome their divisions and visibly manifest their fellowship."[6] Some members of the World Council have even proposed that baptism be declared part of the basis of the organization, or at least that the practice of baptism be made a condition for membership in the World Council.[7]

Initiation is viewed as including the gift of the Holy Spirit: "All (Christians) agree that Christian baptism is in water and the Holy Spirit."[8] Just as the paschal mystery of Christ's death and resurrection cannot be separated from the pentecostal gift of the Holy Spirit, so "participation in Christ's death and resurrection is inseparably linked with the receiving of the Spirit. Baptism in its full meaning signifies and effects both."[9] The exact relationship between baptism and confirmation is acknowledged to be a matter of differing opinion among the churches: "Some churches consider that Christian initiation is not complete without the sealing of the baptized with the gift of the Holy Spirit and participation in holy communion."[10] The 1975 statement offers concrete advice to those churches that understand confirmation as a sacramental completion of baptism but separate it in time from baptism. They could

"(a) reunite baptism and confirmation in a single initiation rite, thus reverting to the practice of the patristic age in the initiation of both adults and children; (b) they could remove confirmation altogether from the basic pattern of admission into the Christian community, interpreting and practising it, for example, as a sacrament of strengthening by the Spirit for mature Christian life. In the second case, they will have to ascribe to water-baptism itself the twofold meaning of incorporation into Christ and participation in his Spirit; otherwise, they will lose sight of an essential aspect of Christian initiation."[11]

Those churches that interpret confirmation nonsacramentally, as an act of personal commitment,

"cannot be said to compromise the sacramental unity of incorporation into Christ and participation in his Spirit. However, if they set a rite of confirmation between baptism and admission to communion, the question arises on what grounds they interpose such a rite. If baptism, as incorporation into the body of Christ, points by its very nature to the eucharistic sharing in Christ's body and blood, on what grounds may a fur-

84

ther rite be interposed? Those churches which baptize children, but refuse them a share in the eucharist before confirmation, may wish to ponder whether they have fully appreciated and accepted the consequences of infant baptism."[12]

These statements reflect years of theological dialogue and have helped immensely in the task of reforming the initiation rites of various churches, particularly in clarifying the relationship between the water-bath and "confirmation." In the process they guarded the unique role of baptism as a once-and-for-all event, while underscoring the need for multiple opportunities throughout the Christian life to reaffirm that baptism.

THE LUTHERAN BOOK OF WORSHIP

The *Lutheran Book of Worship,* issued in 1978,[13] was prepared by the churches participating in the Inter-Lutheran Commission on Worship: Lutheran Church in America, the American Lutheran Church, the Evangelical Lutheran Church of Canada, and the Lutheran Church-Missouri Synod (although this group later withdrew from the joint project and produced its own book). These groups represent all the Lutherans of America, with the exception of a few small, independent groups. Their initiation reform is essentially the same as was seen in the Episcopalian *Book of Common Prayer.* The baptismal sealing follows the water-bath. The minister lays both hands on the head of each of the baptized and prays for the Holy Spirit: "God, the Father of our Lord Jesus Christ, we give you thanks for freeing your sons and daughters from the power of sin and for raising them up to a new life through this holy sacrament. Pour your Holy Spirit upon (name): the spirit of wisdom and understanding, the spirit of counsel and might, the spirit of knowledge and the fear of the Lord, the spirit of joy in your presence."[14] This prayer reflects the one found in the ancient Gelasian

Sacramentary.[15] Then "the minister marks the sign of the cross on the forehead of each of the baptized. Oil prepared for this purpose may be used. As the sign of the cross is made, the minister says: (name), child of God, you have been sealed by the Holy Spirit and marked with the cross of Christ forever."[16] As was seen earlier, this formula is the same as the initial draft attempt of the new Episcopalian rite and has the advantage of not implying that everything is contained in the water-bath alone.

Like the *Book of Common Prayer,* the *Lutheran Book of Worship* retains the term "confirmation" for the first affirmation of one's previous baptism. The same three-fold division is found: confirmation, reception, and restoration to membership (in the *Book of Common Prayer* this is termed "reaffirmation"). Confirmation is described:

"Confirmation marks the completion of the congregation's program of confirmation ministry, a period of instruction in the Christian faith as confessed in the teachings of the Lutheran Church. Those who have completed this program were made members of the Church in Baptism. Confirmation includes a public profession of the faith into which the candidates were baptized, thus underscoring God's action in their Baptism."[17]

A representative of the congregation presents the candidates to the minister saying: "These persons have been instructed in the Christian faith and desire to make public affirmation of their Baptism."[18] The minister lays both hands on the head of each person and prays: "Father in heaven, for Jesus' sake, stir up in (name) the gift of your Holy Spirit; confirm his/her faith, guide his/her life, empower him/her in his/her serving, give him/her patience in suffering, and bring him/her to everlasting life."[19]

86

Luther had strong words for his rejection of the Roman Catholic concept of confirmation. In his *Babylonian Captivity*, published in 1520, he says:

"It is difficult to understand what the Romanists had in mind when they made the sacrament of confirmation out of the laying on of hands. . . . I am not saying this because I condemn the seven sacraments as usages, but because I deny that it can be proved from scripture that these usages are sacraments. O would that there were in the church the kind of laying on of hands that obtained in the time of the apostles, whether we preferred to call it confirmation or healing! But nothing of this remains nowadays except what the Romanists have devised to embellish the duties of bishops, lest they be entirely without function in the church . . . our present inquiry has to do with the nature of the sacraments of divine institution, and we find no reason for enumerating confirmation among them."[20]

Arthur Repp points out that Luther referred to confirmation as monkey business ("Affenspiel"), fanciful deception ("Lügentand"), and mumbo jumbo ("Gaukelwerk").[21]

Luther's concern was that confirmation detracted from baptism, since it was said to complete baptism. He was willing, however, to allow a ceremony of confirmation that stressed the importance of catechetical instruction as preparation for the Lord's Supper. Repp explains that "confirmation did not play an important role in his [Luther's] thoughts. His interest took a different tack. He was concerned primarily with catechetical instruction."[22] Thus in the Lutheran tradition confirmation is intimately tied to the Word. Repp summarizes:

"During the major portion of the Lutheran Church's history, confirmation was not universally observed with a ceremony. The heart of confirmation lies in the instruction in the Word that precedes the rite. The real confirmation takes place in the confirmation of faith by the Word, for through the Word God continues to confirm the faith begun in Baptism and nurtured by the home and the church. . . . The word confirm should be used not for anything the catechumens do but for what God does. When the term is used in referring to the pastor or congregation as the one who confirms, it is used only in a derived sense; pastor and congregation act under God's command."[23]

The Lutheran Church-Missouri Synod took exception to a number of elements in the *Lutheran Book of Worship* and so produced its own *Lutheran Worship* in 1982.[24] In its service of Holy Baptism there is no signing or anointing after the water-bath but only an imposition of hand and blessing: "The minister lays his hand upon the one baptized and gives this blessing: Almighty God, the Father of our Lord Jesus Christ, who has given you the new birth of water and of the Spirit and has forgiven you all your sins, strengthen you with his grace to life everlasting. Peace be with you."[25] In lieu of the section on "Affirmation of Baptism" (which is divided into three categories) in the *Lutheran Book of Worship,* The Missouri Synod entitles the section "Confirmation," with no subcategories. Although this rite of confirmation is intended for those already baptized who now are to confess their baptismal faith, they are strangely referred to as "catechumens," a marked departure from the traditional custom of reserving that word for those preparing for baptism, not for confirmation.

UNITED METHODIST: ALTERNATE TEXT 1976
The reforms of the initiation rites of the United Methodist Church took place in an ecumenical context. In dialogue with the Episcopalians, Lutherans, and others, the United Methodists examined patristic sources and rethought the biblical witness of the earliest ecclesial traditions. The result was the alternate text of 1976, *A Service of Baptism, Confirmation, and Renewal.*[26]

While John Wesley was, of course, marked by his Anglican background, he did make certain innovations in his teaching concerning baptism and regeneration. For example, as Bernard Holland writes:

"One common feature of Anglican devotion in the eighteenth century was the calling to mind and renewal of the vow made at baptism. But, as we have noticed, Wesley made no use of this devotional aid, for he considered that the baptismal covenant is so irreparably broken by sin that what is required is not its renewal but the making of a new covenant: the sinner must make a new start with God, and for this his past baptism is of no consequence."[27]

For Wesley, serious sin after infant baptism was inevitable and obliterated the benefits received in infant baptism. It began at about the age of nine or ten. Thus, regeneration is offered to all at two stages of life: in infancy (baptism) and in adulthood (conversion).[28]

Laurence Stookey describes the development of the baptismal rites in American Methodism during the twentieth century most astutely:

"One can hardly miss the shift within a quarter of a century from original guilt theology, to covenant theology with an implied universalism, to a rather explicit universalism, to an almost blatant humanism. By the final stage, it is exceedingly unclear in the entire rite (not merely in the general address) what God does in baptism, if anything. But it is rather evident that baptism has nothing to do with sin, inherited or actual.
. . . While the American Methodists of the early twentieth century may have been more given to tinkering with their liturgies than were other denominations, they were by no means alone in their confusion and perplexity. In a number of Protestant denominations (including the Methodist) the baptism of infants came to be rejected by some people in favor of a service of

'dedication of infants.' This was not based on a well-thought-out view of baptism as the sacramental initiation rite for the mature, but simply upon an inability to find any defensible meaning in baptism as a sacrament. The streams of revivalism-pentecostalism and of liberalism converged with disastrous results."[29]

Facing up to this situation, the initiation reform of 1976 is well thought out. After the water-bath the minister places hands on those receiving baptism and says: "The power of the Holy Spirit work within you, that being born through water and the Spirit you may be a faithful witness of Jesus Christ. Amen."[30] Thus, like the liturgy of the *Book of Common Prayer*, the traditional sealing here is in the context of baptism. Unlike the Episcopalian practice, no consignation is found, only the imposition of hands. The "Commentary on the Text" states: "Among those who place hands upon the newly baptized may be the following persons: minister, parents and other family members, sponsors, lay leader or other representative who has presented the candidate, and others who may be gathered at the font. In particular, when the family unit includes baptized children, these children should be encouraged to share in the act."[31]

While baptism is a once-and-for-all event, the ritual offers various possibilities for the renewal of the baptismal covenant.

"For those who have been baptized as infants or children, there is a significant first occurrence of such renewal, commonly called 'confirmation.' The title is appropriate on two counts: First, in this rite, God confirms his promise to those who were too young to understand that promise at the time of their baptism. Second, these persons confirm their personal commitment in a public testimony they were unable to make as infants or children. Through this double confirmation, faith and dedication are strengthened."[32]

The ritual of confirmation and other renewals of the baptismal covenant is described as follows:

"Water may be sprinkled toward: all persons being confirmed, or persons making a special renewal of their baptismal faith, or the entire congregation when there is a general renewal of baptismal faith. The minister says: 'Remember your Baptism and be thankful. Amen.' As hands are placed upon the head of each person being confirmed or making a special renewal, the minister says: '(name), the power of the Holy Spirit work within you, that, having been born through water and the Spirit, you may continue to be a faithful witness of Jesus Christ. Amen.' "[33]

While the term "confirmation" is reserved for the first renewal of the baptismal faith of those baptized in infancy or childhood, nevertheless provision is made for special renewal (on the part of specific individuals) and general renewal (by the entire worshiping assembly of baptized persons). General renewal is especially fitting on the Sunday after the Epiphany, which is known as the Sunday of the Baptism of the Lord, and at the Easter Vigil. These renewals, both specific and general, are most important "for although God does not forget his promises to us, we do tend to forget them; and in times of stress we may doubt the truth of his promises even if we do not forget their existence. Furthermore, we frequently neglect the obligations placed upon us in the baptismal covenant. For these reasons it is appropriate for every Christian to renew the baptismal covenant from time to time."[34] The United Methodist rite, unlike the Episcopalian and Lutheran rites, uses the laying on of hands not only for confirmation proper but for all the acts of renewal, although in rites of corporate renewal hands are not laid on the entire congregation.

The Presbyterian Church in the United States and the United Presbyterian Church in the United States of America have merged to form the Presbyterian Church (U.S.A.). Their initiation reforms appear in *The Plan for Renunion*.[35]

Like Luther, Calvin felt that confirmation detracts from baptism. His words about confirmation are strong, to say the least: "I regard it as one of the most deadly wiles of Satan," and again, "Confirmation is oil polluted with falsehood of the devil, to darken and deceive the minds of the simple."[36] Calvin's words must be interpreted in light of the fact that he was speaking against the rite of confirmation of his day. He felt that it had existed previously in a purer form by which young people professed their baptismal faith:

"I sincerely wish that we retained the custom, which I have stated was practised among the ancients before this abortive image of a sacrament made its appearance. For it was not such a confirmation as the Romanists pretend, which cannot be mentioned without injury to baptism; but a catechetical exercise, in which children or youths used to deliver an account of their faith in the presence of the church."[37]

The direction taken in *The Plan for Reunion* approved by the two merging church bodies in 1982 is not exactly that which we have seen among the Episcopalians, Lutherans, and United Methodists. Any mention of confirmation has been omitted. The water-bath is to be accompanied by no other ceremony. Thus, some may criticize the incompleteness of the rite. The World Council statement recommends in this regard: "It would seem appropriate that baptism with water should be followed by the laying-on of hands or chrismation to express dedication and the gift of the Holy Spirit in baptism."[38] According to *The Plan for Reunion*, baptism, which is to be administered only once, may be used for either infants or consenting believers. It heralds a participation in the ministry of Christ:

"Such participation initiated in baptism then becomes an ever-expanding process, setting Christians on a journey which lasts the whole course of their lives. As the baptism of Jesus anticipated the whole course of his obedience, so the meaning of one's own baptism becomes apparent only through the subsequent course of one's life as one practices what it means to be the Lord's in changing situations and in new relationships."[39]

The section on "The Sacraments" ends with a treatment of the Lord's Supper. Then follows a section entitled "Admission to Active Membership." It is similar to the three categories set by The *Book of Common Prayer* in that "persons may become active Church members in the following ways: by profession of faith, reaffirmation of faith in Jesus Christ, or transfer of certificate from some other church."[40] Those baptized in infancy are invited at a later point in their lives to profess publicly their faith; but unlike the Episcopalian, Lutheran, and Methodist rites it is not called confirmation, nor is there any laying on of hands. It is interesting that the section "The Lord's Supper" includes among those invited to partake in the sacrament baptized children who have not yet made their public profession of faith.[41]

CONCLUSION

These denominations have been chosen as a cross-section of initiation reforms among Protestant churches. They exemplify and embody the concern of the past fifty years of the Faith and Order Commission of the World Council of Churches. As with the new rites of the Episcopalian *Book of Common Prayer* these reforms are precisely "rites of initiation," rites celebrating entrance into a faith community. These rites celebrate a twofold given reality: first, the gratuitous gift of God's claim on us in the context of a Spirit-filled community, and second, the periodic affirmation of that gift during life's journey in the Spirit.

The Anglican and Protestant reforms contribute to an awareness that Roman Catholics frequently join together two different things under the title of confirmation: the hand-laying with the associated rites accompanying the water-bath in the early life of the church and the renewal of that baptismal covenant at a later time in life. In spite of forcing confirmation to bear these conflicting meanings, Catholics have always seen confirmation (at least in principle) in its relationship to baptism. But in fact, the nature of that relationship has often remained obscure. A penetrating insight has been shed on the matter by the new *Rite of Christian Initiation of Adults:*

"According to the ancient practice maintained in the Roman liturgy, an adult is not to be baptized unless he receives confirmation immediately afterward, provided no serious obstacles exist. This connection signifies the unity of the paschal mystery, the close relationship between the mission of the Son and the pouring out of the Holy Spirit, and the joint celebration of the sacraments by which the Son and the Spirit come with the Father upon those who are baptized" [34].

NOTES

1. *One Baptism, One Eucharist and a Mutually Recognized Ministry,* Faith and Order Paper 73 (World Council of Churches, Geneva 1975). *Baptism, Eucharist and Ministry,* Faith and Order Paper 111 (World Council of Churches, Geneva 1982).

2. *Baptism* (1975), no. 2.

3. *Baptism* (1982), no. 4.

4. Ibid., no. 10.

5. *Baptism* (1975), no. 5.

6. *Baptism* (1982), no. 6.

7. See Avery Dulles, "Toward a Christian Consensus: The Lima Meeting," *America* 146 (1982), p. 129.

8. *Baptism* (1982), no. 14.

9. Ibid.

10. Ibid., no. 20.

11. *Baptism* (1975), no. 17.

12. Ibid., no. 18.

13. *Lutheran Book of Worship* (Augsburg, Minneapolis 1978).

14. Ibid., p. 124.

15. See E. C. Whitaker, *Documents of the Baptismal Liturgy* (SPCK, London 1970), p. 195.

16. *Lutheran Book of Worship*, p. 124. The water-bath, the laying on of hands, and the signing are not considered three separate actions, but "one rich action of initiation." See Philip H. Pfatteicher and Carlos R. Messerli, *Manual on the Liturgy: Lutheran Book of Worship* (Augsburg, Minneapolis 1979), p. 185.

17. Ibid., p. 198.

18. Ibid.

19. Ibid., p. 201. See Pfatteicher and Messerli, pp. 339–345.

20. As quoted in J. D. C. Fisher, *Christian Initiation: The Reformation Period* (SPCK, London 1970), p. 171.

21. See Arthur C. Repp, *Confirmation in the Lutheran Church* (Concordia, St. Louis 1964), p. 15.

22. Ibid., p. 18.

23. Ibid., pp. 177–178.

24. *Lutheran Worship* (Concordia, St. Louis 1982).

25. Ibid., p. 203.

26. *A Service of Baptism, Confirmation, and Renewal,* Supplemental Worship Resources 2 (Parthenon Press, Nashville, 1976, rev. ed. 1980).

27. Bernard G. Holland, *Baptism in Early Methodism* (Epworth Press, London 1970), pp. 74–75.

28. See ibid., pp. 72–83.

29. Laurence H. Stookey, *Baptism: Christ's Act in the Church* (Abingdon Press, Nashville 1982), pp. 131–132.

30. *A Service of Baptism, Confirmation, and Renewal,* pp. 17–18.

31. Ibid., pp. 24–25.

32. Ibid., p. 11.

33. Ibid., p. 18.

34. Ibid., p. 12.

35. *The Plan for Reunion* prepared by Joint Committee on Presbyterian Union, N.Y., final edition 1981.

36. As quoted in Fisher, pp. 254–255.

37. Ibid., p. 258.

38. *Baptism* (1975), no. 19.

39. *The Plan for Reunion,* p. 250.

40. Ibid., p. 263.

41. Ibid., p. 259: "The invitation shall include baptized children who are being nurtured and instructed to participate with an understanding of the significance of the invitation to the Lord's Table and of their response in faith."

Chapter Five

Rite of the Blessing of Oils;
Rite of Consecrating Chrism

*Rite of the Blessing of Oils; Rite of Consecrating the
Chrism* was published in 1971.[1] The Congregation for
Divine Worship had authorized the rite on December 3,
1970.[2] The revision represents a rearrangement and
simplification of the prayers of blessing of oils and
consecration of chrism. Since "the blessing of the oil
and the consecration of the chrism are ordinarily celebrated by the bishop at the chrism Mass celebrated on
Holy Thursday morning" [9], the rite should not be
considered by itself but must be viewed in its proper
and larger liturgical frame, the new rites of Holy Week.
The consecration of the chrism is reserved to the bishop
alone [6], and ordinarily the blessing of the oils is also
to be done by him [7–9]; therefore, the new rite is to be
inserted into the liturgical book of the bishop, the Pontifical.

Since both the oil of catechumens and chrism are to be
used in initiation rites, the introduction reflects this
context: "Catechumens are prepared and disposed for
baptism" with the oil of catechumens [1]. "By the oil of
catechumens the effect of the baptismal exorcisms is
extended" [2]. "By confirmation Christians receive the
spiritual anointing of the Spirit who is given to them"
[2]. The perennial problem of the relationship between
the postbaptismal anointing and the sacrament of
confirmation is touched on by the choice of words
"anointed and confirmed": "The newly baptized are
anointed and confirmed with the chrism consecrated by

97

the bishop" [1]. Finally, the oil of the sick is described as follows: "By the use of the oil of the sick, to which Saint James is a witness, the sick received a remedy for the illness of mind and body, so that they may have strength to bear suffering and resist evil and obtain the forgiveness of sins" [2].[3]

HISTORICAL SURVEY
The historical development of chrism and oils in Christian communities is fascinating. The early church's use of oil was influenced, although not determined, by the pagan and secular use of oil in antiquity, and by the Old Testament typologies.[4] The secular use of oil included the bath, where oil held the place that soap does in modern life, and the gymnasium, where athletes oiled themselves for games and exercises. Pagan religious rites imitated those usages of health and sport, and oil was freely used, especially in conjunction with sacrifice. Leonel Mitchell observes:

". . . we can see the importance which oil had in the life of the average Roman. Not only did he cook with it, burn it in his lamps, and wash with it, but he used it as a medicine, as a cosmetic, and in religious rites. The association of washing and anointing was extremely close both in religious ceremonial and in daily life. Certainly the idea of a sacred anointing would not have been alien to the mind of a neophyte coming to the Church from the pagan Roman world."[5]

Frequent references to oil in the Old Testament greatly influenced Christian interpretation and usage. In Exodus we read the Lord's command for making this "holy oil": "Take the finest spices: of liquid myrrh five hundred shekels, and of sweet-smelling cinnamon half as much, that is, two hundred and fifty, and of aromatic cane two hundred and fifty, and of cassia five hundred, according to the shekel of the sanctuary, and of olive oil a hin; and you shall make of these a sacred

98

anointing oil blended as by the perfumer; a holy anointing oil it shall be" (Ex 30:23–25). Oil was employed not only for persons but for things as well. Jacob poured oil over the stone at Bethel (Gn 28:18). A warrior's shield might be anointed (Is 21:5). The tabernacle and its furniture were consecrated by an anointing with oil (Ex 30:26–28). Most important, oil was used in anointing kings (1 Sm 10:1, 16:13; 2 Kgs 9:6, 11:12, 23:30), prophets (1 Kgs 19:16; Is 61:1–2), and priests (Ex 28:41, 29:7; Lv 8:12; Nm 3:3). The anointing makes the king or priest a sacred person, the "anointed of the Lord," which in Hebrew is "the Messiah" and in Greek "the Christ." The anointing of David in 1 Samuel 16:13 is important: "Then Samuel took the horn of oil, and anointed him in the midst of his brothers; and *the Spirit of the Lord came mightly upon David* from that day forward" (italics mine). The psalms often speak of David and his dynasty as the "Anointed." He was the prototype of the King, the Messiah to come. The New Testament applies the title to Jesus, who is "the Christ." Peter's confession of Jesus, reflecting the more developed faith of the primitive Christian community, states: "You are the Christ" (Mk 8:29).

To understand the Christian usage of oils it is important to remember that the full understanding of the symbol is derived not so much from the cultural use and natural symbolism of oil as from biblical history, where the definitive signification is connected with Jesus' being the Anointed One. Luke regards Jesus' own baptism by John in the Jordan as an "anointing with the Spirit" (Acts 10:38). The Christian is called to enter into, to share in, that anointing. The author of 1 John says: "You have been anointed by the Holy One" (1 Jn 2:20).

As was seen earlier, scholars dispute whether the various mentionings of "anointing" in the New Testament are to be taken literally (as an actual rite of anointing) or metaphorically (as a way of indicating our participation in the messianic unction of Christ). Raymond Brown thinks that the anointing of the baptismal ceremony mentioned in the Acts of the Apostles does not mean an actual exterior rite of anointing at the time of baptism, but "simply a figurative way of describing the effects of baptism."[6] Nevertheless, very early in Christian history we do know that such actual anointings were performed as part of the baptismal ceremony. The earliest treatise we have on baptism is Tertullian's *De Baptismo*, written about the year A.D. 200, and chapter 7 describes the postbaptismal ceremonies:

"After that we come up from the washing and are anointed with the blessed unction, following that ancient practice by which, ever since Aaron was anointed by Moses, there was a custom of anointing them for priesthood with oil out of a horn. That is why (the high priest) is called a christ, from 'chrism' which is (the Greek for) 'anointing': and from this also our Lord obtained his title, though it had become a spiritual anointing, in that he was anointed with the Spirit by God the Father: and so (it says) in the Acts, 'For of a truth they are gathered together in this city against thy holy Son whom thou has anointed.' So also in our case, the unction flows upon the flesh, but turns to spiritual profit, just as in the baptism itself there is an act that touches the flesh, that we are immersed in water, but a spiritual effect, that we are set free from sins."[7]

Our richest and most important source of information for the use of oil in early baptismal ceremonies is the *Apostolic Tradition*, written by Hippolytus around the year 215.[8] Here we find two kinds of oil: "oil of exorcism," which the bishop has exorcised, and "oil of thanksgiving," over which he has given thanks.[9] The former is used before baptism (as is our oil of catechumens today), and the latter is used twice after the water-bath, once by a presbyter and once by the bishop (as our chrism is used today). Hippolytus does not provide us with the actual words of exorcism or thanksgiving prayed over the oils. He does give us, however, the formulas used in applying the oils. Before the baptism a presbyter anoints with the oil of exorcism, saying: "May every evil spirit depart from you."[10] Immediately after the water-bath a presbyter anoints the body of the candidate with the oil of thanksgiving, saying: "I anoint you with holy oil in the name of Jesus Christ."[11] Finally, the newly baptized is brought to the bishop. The bishop imposes his hand upon him, prays, and then anoints his head saying: "I anoint you with holy oil in God the Father Almighty, and in Christ Jesus, and in the Holy Spirit."[12] This practice described by Hippolytus is important because it becomes the "Roman model": prebaptismal anointing of exorcism and a double postbaptismal anointing, one by a presbyter and one by the bishop.

While terminology varied in different regions, oil (*oleum*) was originally olive oil and chrism (*chrisma*) was perfumed oil. In the East a large variety of perfumes were added, and thus the oil was called *myron* (perfume). By the year 390, the Second Council of Carthage, in Canon 3, restricted the consecration of the chrism to the bishop; the same practice was followed in the East, except that there the consecration eventually became the sole prerogative of the patriarch.[13]

It is the perfume that constitutes the essence of the symbolism of chrism, and this chrism is revered as something holy. Indeed, the chrism in a certain way contains the Holy Spirit, as Cyril of Jerusalem (d. 386) says of the perfumed oil, the *myron:*

"But beware of supposing this to be plain ointment. For as the Bread of the Eucharist, after the invocation of the Holy Ghost, is mere bread no longer, but the Body of Christ, so also this holy ointment is no more simple ointment, or (so to say) common, after the invocation, but the gift of Christ; and by the presence of His Godhead, it causes in us the Holy Ghost. It is symbolically applied to thy forehead and thy other senses; and while thy body is anointed with visible ointment, thy soul is sanctified by the Holy and life-giving Spirit."[14]

In the *Apostolic Constitutions* of the late fourth or early fifth centuries the chrism clearly bears the role of continuing the sweet odor of Christ:

"And after this, when he has baptized him in the Name of the Father and of the Son and of the Holy Ghost, let him anoint him with chrism, and say: O Lord God, who art without generation, and without a superior, the Lord of the whole world, who hast scattered the sweet odour of the knowledge of the gospel among all nations, do thou grant at this time that this chrism may be efficacious upon him that is baptized, so that the sweet odour of thy Christ may continue upon him firm and fixed; and that now he has died with him, he may arise and live with him."[15]

THE LITURGY OF THE OILS AND CHRISM

While the oil of the sick was ordinarily blessed right before the end of the eucharistic prayer, the blessing of the oil of catechumens and the consecration of chrism took place after communion, that is, between the communion of the pope or bishop and the communion of the people.[16] This was first done at the Easter Vigil; but by the sixth century in both East and West this action had been transferred to Holy Thursday, probably to lighten the ceremonies of the Easter Vigil. Some places, like Paris, however, blessed the oils on Palm Sunday (hence the name for that Sunday, *dies unctionis*) while other places, like Arles, retained the primitive practice of blessing the oils at the Easter Vigil.[17] The papal *Ordo XXIII* for Holy Thursday, which describes the seventh-century practice, mentions only the chrism.[18] The other two oils, the oil of catechumens and the oil of the sick, could be blessed either by the pope or by priests in parish churches.[19] In the Eastern churches the prebaptismal oil and the oil of the sick are to this day blessed by the priest at the time they are to be used.

The rite of consecration of chrism, like the eucharist itself, was concelebrated. It was done in a silent way, that is, the priests gathered around the bishop and extended their right hands toward the vessel containing the chrism, while the bishop alone pronounced the prayer of consecration.

From the sixth to the eighth centuries, the simple Roman liturgy of blessing of oils was transplanted into Gaul and, as happened to so many elements of the liturgy, was made more complex there, as is reflected in the chrism mass of the Gelasian Sacramentary.[20] In addition to the traditional Roman prayer for the consecration of the chrism, the Gallican usage here added the exorcism prayer for the oil of catechumens and mistakenly applied it to the chrism. For the preface of the chrism mass, it used an ancient Gallican prayer for the consecration of the chrism.[21] This great prayer of consecration of the chrism found in the Gelasian Sacramentary is basically that which has been in use for 1,300 years in the Roman church. It is "form A" of the 1970 rite. In the Gelasian it had the pattern of a preface, but today it has been given the form of a prayer.

The compiler of the Romano-Germanic Pontifical of the Tenth Century made further changes in the blessing of the oils.[22] The oils are brought in procession, carried by the bishop, to the chant of "O Redeemer." At least twelve priests are to be involved, and they are called *testes et cooperatores eiusdem sacrosancti chrismalis misterii.*[23] The 1970 rite echoes this profound truth of priestly involvement: "It is desirable that there be some priests from the various sections of the diocese among the priests who concelebrate with the bishop and are his witnesses and co-workers in the ministry of the holy chrism" [14].

The tenth-century liturgy has the bishop breathe over the chrism three times. The 1970 rite echoes this by saying immediately before the consecratory prayer of the chrism: "Then the bishop may breathe over the opening of the vessel of chrism" [25]. Finally, the compiler of the Romano-Germanic Pontifical of the Tenth Century confused the situation by adding to the traditional Roman prayer of consecration the Gallican preface for the chrism mass. Fortunately, the 1955 reform of Holy Week separated these two things, and returned the Gallican addition to its rightful place as the preface of the mass.

Further medieval changes were made by William Durand, bishop of Mende (d. 1296). He had the priests join the bishop in breathing on the chrism, and had an elaborate closing ceremony that included the priests kissing the vessel containing the chrism.[24]

During the Middle Ages there was, at least at times, a great sense of reverence felt toward the chrism. In the thirteenth century there was a widespread practice of placing a white band around one's forehead after confirmation. The chrism was not to be left just "open" on a person's forehead. On the third day after the confirmation ceremony the newly confirmed were to be brought to the church so that the priest might remove the band, wash away any remaining chrism, and burn the chrismal cloth out of reverence. A number of church councils of the thirteenth century passed legislation on this point.[25] The practice is probably rooted in Christian antiquity since it is found also in the Christian East, in Syria and Armenia. Perhaps it has its roots in the baptismal theology of the primitive church, which included the theme of priestly crowning. A history of this interesting practice of confirmation bands still remains to be written.

THE NEW RITE

The 1970 reform of the rite of blessing oils and consecrating chrism attempts to underscore the essentials of the rite, sometimes using elements from the past, sometimes creating new elements. Out of concern for places in the world where olive oil is scarce, one may now use other plant oil [3]. Out of concern for the pastoral difficulty of getting people together on Holy Thursday morning, "the blessing may be held on an earlier day, near Easter, with the celebration of the proper chrism Mass" [10]. The blessing is often held on one of the days at the beginning of Holy Week. Wednesday evening of that week might be a good choice.

Following ancient custom, the blessing of the oil of the sick takes place before the end of the eucharistic prayer while the blessing of the oil of catechumens and the consecration of the chrism occurs after communion [11]. "For pastoral reasons, however, the entire rite of blessing may be celebrated after the liturgy of the word" [12]. Perhaps what is being implied here is that there would be a pastoral advantage of blessing the oils immediately after the homily, in which a catechesis would be given, explaining the action of the blessing of the oils.

The blessing of the oil of the sick in the new rite was the work of the commission that prepared the *Rite of Anointing and Pastoral Care of the Sick*. They did away with the former exorcism prayer and also omitted the element of the blessing that had confused the oil of the sick with chrism by making mention of the anointing of kings, priest, prophets, and martyrs.[26] The new prayer asks: "May your blessing come upon all who are

105

anointed with this oil, that they may be freed from pain and illness and made well again in body, mind, and soul" [20].

After the communion of the chrism mass, the oil of catechumens is blessed by the bishop. "In the case of the baptism of adults, however, priests have the faculty to bless the oil of catechumens before the anointing in the designated stage of the catechumenate" [7].[27] The blessing prayer here for the oil of catechumens is entirely new and was the work of the committee entrusted with the reform of the initiation rites. As mentioned previously, for Hippolytus this oil was the "oil of exorcism."

The variety of meanings of the prebaptismal anointing was extremely rich in the early church. St. Cyril of Jerusalem says:

"Then, when you were stripped, you were anointed with exorcized oil, from the very hairs of your head, to your feet, and were made partakers of the good olive tree, Jesus Christ. For you were cut off from the wild olive-tree, and grafted into the good one, and were made to share the fatness of the true olive-tree. The exorcized oil therefore was a symbol of the participation in the fatness of Christ, the charm to drive away every trace of hostile influence. For as the breathing of the saints, and the invocation of the Name of God, like fiercest flame, scorch and drive out evil spirits, so also this exorcized oil receives such virtue by the invocation of God and by prayer, as not only to burn and cleanse away the traces of sins, but also to chase away all the invisible powers of the evil one."[28]

Hugh Riley analyzes the different interpretations given by certain early church Fathers to the body-anointing before the baptismal bath and discerns three key themes: the exorcistic-healing motif, the combat motif, and the motif of union with Christ.[29] Gabriele Winkler

106

shows that there are two basic aspects involved in the early prebaptismal anointing: one positive (pneumatic in orientation involving the bestowal of the Holy Spirit and union with Christ) and the other negative (apotropaic and exorcistic in orientation).[30]

One wonders if, in the light of such a rich past, the new blessing prayer is not an impoverishment: "Lord God, protector of all who believe in you, bless this oil and give wisdom and strength to all who are anointed with it in preparation for their baptism. Bring them to a deeper understanding of the gospel, help them to accept the challenge of Christian living, and lead them to the joy of new birth in the family of your Church. We ask this through Christ our Lord. R. Amen" [22]. Granted that modern Christians have lost the profound awareness of evil, and thus of exorcisms, it may well be asked if the evils of egoism and violence and injustice that the newly baptized must encounter are not equally forgotten. Perhaps the Latin phrase in the blessing, *magno animo labores vitae christianae aggrediantur*, should have been translated much more forcefully than "help them to accept the challenge of Christian living."

THE CONSECRATION OF CHRISM
After the blessing of the oil of catechumens comes the consecration of chrism. "Then the bishop pours the balsam or perfume in the oil and mixes the chrism in silence, unless this was done beforehand" [23]. The bishop then intones an invitation to pray, breathes over the opening of the vessel of chrism, extends his hands, and says the consecratory prayer. Two forms are given, the first of which is the traditional one that has been in use since the seventh century.[31] Here, however, it is put in the form of a prayer rather than in the traditional form of a preface:

"God our maker,
source of all growth in holiness,
accept the joyful thanks and praise
we offer in the name of your Church.

In the beginning, at your command,
the earth produced fruit-bearing trees.
From the fruit of the olive tree
you have provided us with oil for holy chrism.
The prophet David sang of the life and joy
that the oil would bring us in the sacraments of your
  love.

After the avenging flood,
the dove returning to Noah with an olive branch
announced your gift of peace.
This was a sign of a greater gift to come.
Now the waters of baptism wash away the sins of
  men,
and by anointing with olive oil
you make us radiant with your joy.

At your command,
Aaron was washed with water,
and your servant Moses, his brother,
anointed him priest.
This too foreshadowed greater things to come.
After your Son, Jesus Christ our Lord,
asked John for baptism in the waters of Jordan,
you sent the Spirit upon him
in the form of a dove
and by the witness of your own voice
you declared him to be your only, well-beloved Son.
In this you clearly fulfilled the prophecy of David,
that Christ would be anointed with the oil of gladness
beyond his fellow men.

All the celebrants extend their right hands toward the
chrism, without saying anything, until the end of the
prayer.

And so, Father, we ask you to bless ✠ this oil you
    have created.
Fill it with the power of your Holy Spirit
through Christ your Son.
It is from him that chrism takes its name
and with chrism you have anointed
for yourself priests and kings,
prophets and martyrs.

Make this chrism a sign of life and salvation
for those who are to be born again in the waters of
    baptism.
Wash away the evil they have inherited from sinful
    Adam,
and when they are anointed with this holy oil
make them temples of your glory,
radiant with the goodness of life
that has its source in you.

Through this sign of chrism
grant them royal, priestly and prophetic honor,
and clothe them with incorruption.
Let this be indeed the chrism of salvation
for those who will be born again of water and the Holy
    Spirit.
May they come to share eternal life
in the glory of your kingdom.
We ask this through Christ our Lord.
R. Amen" [25].

This prayer of consecration is an ideal source for development of a theology of chrismal anointing.[32] Rich in
Old Testament typology, it reaches its crescendo in
Christ, the Anointed One: "It is from him that chrism
takes its name." The theme of the deluge and reconciliation find their resolution in the Jordan event. Through
baptism Christians partake of this mystery, and they,
too, receive the anointing of the Holy Spirit, the Spirit
who is the gift. This gift of the Spirit is a pledge of

salvation. Paul writes to the Corinthians, "He has put his seal upon us and gives us his Spirit in our hearts as a guarantee" (2 Cor 1:22). The prayer says, "Let this be indeed the chrism of salvation for those who will be born again of water and the Holy Spirit." In the baptismal context, "being born again" of John 3:5 is a question of a gift that both leads to a life of faith and comes from a life of faith. The life of faith is a life according to the Spirit.[33] This life, by its very nature, leads the baptized to its completion, where the guarantee, the pledge (*arrabōn*), will be given in full; so the consecratory prayer ends, "May they come to share eternal life in the glory of your kingdom."

The second form of the consecratory prayer is entirely new. It was thought desirable to have another prayer in use that would place greater stress on the paschal mystery and on the church:

"Father, we thank you for the gifts
you have given us in your love:
we thank you for life itself and for the sacraments
that strengthen it and give it fuller meaning.

In the Old Covenant you gave your people
a glimpse of the power of this holy oil
and when the fullness of time had come
you brought that mystery to perfection
in the life of our Lord Jesus Christ, your Son.

By his suffering, dying, and rising to life
he saved the human race.
He sent your Spirit to fill the Church
with every gift needed to complete your saving work.

From that time forward,
through the sign of holy chrism,
you dispense your life and love to men.
By anointing them with the Spirit,
you strengthen all who have been reborn in baptism.

Through that anointing
you transform them into the likeness of Christ your
   Son
and give them a share
in his royal, priestly, and prophetic work.

All the concelebrants extend their right hands toward the
chrism without saying anything, until the end of the
prayer.

And so, Father, by the power of your love,
make this mixture of oil and perfume
a sign and source ✠ of your blessing.
Pour out the gifts of your Holy Spirit
on our brothers and sisters who will be anointed
   with it.
Let the splendor of holiness shine on the world
from every place and thing
signed with this oil.

Above all, Father, we pray
that through this sign of your anointing
you will grant increase to your Church
until it reaches the eternal glory
where you, Father, will be the all in all,
together with Christ your Son,
in the unity of the Holy Spirit,
for ever and ever.
R. Amen" [25].

Chrism functions here in the context of a church that is
Spirit-filled. The lines, "Let the splendor of holiness
shine on the world from every place and thing signed
with this oil," are a reminder that chrism is used not
only for anointing men and women, but for anointing
such things as churches and altars as well.

For a full understanding of the prayers of consecration
of chrism one must remember the total liturgical context, and in particular, the Scripture readings provided

for the chrism mass, because liturgical blessings are a response to God's word. In the gospel (Lk 4:16–21) Jesus attributes to himself the passage of Isaiah that had been used as the first reading: "The Spirit of the Lord is upon me, because he has anointed me to preach good news to the poor. He has sent me to proclaim release to the captives and recovering of sight to the blind, to set at liberty those who are oppressed, to proclaim the acceptable year of the Lord" Lk 4:18–19). The second reading (Rv 1:5–8) reminds Christians that they have been made "a kingdom, priests to his God and Father" (Rv 1:6).

RENEWAL OF PRIESTLY COMMITMENT
During the early Middle Ages, as the Gelasian Sacramentary shows, there were three masses provided for Holy Thursday: a mass for the reconciliation of penitents, the chrism mass, and an evening mass commemorating the Last Supper.[34] This practice probably represents that of the parish churches of Rome. But early in the seventh century, the papal practice at the Lateran knew only one mass on Holy Thursday, and during this mass the pope blessed the chrism.

Today there are two: the chrism mass and the mass of the Lord's Supper. According to the *Revised Rites of Holy Week* the mass of the Lord's Supper is to be celebrated in the evening. "The homily should explain the principal mysteries which are commemorated in this mass: the institution of the eucharist, the institution of the priesthood, and Christ's commandment of brotherly love."[35] The chrism mass itself, as mentioned earlier, could be held on an earlier day, near Easter, if there was difficulty in gathering the assembly on Holy Thursday morning. The traditional focus of this liturgy has always been the blessing of the oils and the consecration of the chrism, with the chrism holding primacy of place.

Pope Paul VI added something totally new: the "Renewal of Commitment to Priestly Service," to take place after the homily. The danger in this addition is that it risks throwing attention off the chrism and putting undue emphasis on the ordained priesthood to the detriment of the priesthood of all believers. In other words, it runs the risk of clericalizing the chrism mass.[36] Granted that chrism is used as part of the liturgy of ordination of priests and bishops; nevertheless, the primary symbolism of chrism pertains to Christian initiation, to becoming a Christian, a serious and important point of liturgy and ecclesiology. Liturgy must not belie belief. The ordained priesthood can only be truly understood in the larger context of the priesthood of all believers, that is, in that priesthood of baptism that is shared by both laity and clergy alike. This truth is often forgotten, as in the case when some laity believe that they are not worthy to receive communion in the hand because only the priest's hands are anointed. They forget that they have been anointed with the Spirit in their own sacraments of initiation. Raymond Brown writes: "I think that this priesthood of all believers will present a challenge in the church of our times. In particular, the next twenty years will see a special struggle on the part of ordained priests as they come to grips with the implications of the priesthood of all believers."[37]

J. Frank Henderson rightly points out that the risk of clericalizing the chrism mass begins with the very opening prayer, which is worded: "Father, by the power of the Holy Spirit you anointed your only Son Messiah and Lord of creation; you have given us a share in his consecration to priestly service in your Church. Help us to be faithful witnesses in the world to the salvation Christ won for all mankind." Henderson comments: "My question regarding this prayer is, to whom does the 'us' refer? That is, who can fully

participate in the praying of this text; is it a prayer of
the entire eucharistic assembly, or is it a prayer of the
ordained priests alone?"[38] This point is important, as
the presidential prayers, although said by the priest
celebrant, are pronounced in the name of all. The *Constitution on the Sacred Liturgy* says, "The prayers addressed to God by the priest, who presides over the
assembly in the person of Christ, are said in the name
of the entire holy people and of all present."[39]

This new phenomenon, the clericalization of the chrism
mass, is even more striking and ambiguous when one
remembers that the three scripture readings provided
for the chrism mass are in reference to the priesthood
of the entire people of God: Isaiah 61:1–3, 6, 8–9;
Revelation 1:5–8; Luke 4:16–21.

DEDICATION OF A CHURCH
Another use of oil and chrism in the liturgy is when a
church and altar are dedicated. The new rite, *Ordo
Dedicationis Ecclesiae et Altaris,* was promulgated by the
Congregation for Sacraments and Divine Worship on
May 29, 1977.[40] The rite, which is still in provisional
text form, is part of the Roman Pontifical and contains:
laying of the foundation stone or beginning of work on
a new church; dedication of a church; dedication of an
altar; blessing of a church; blessing of an altar; blessing
of a chalice and paten. Kevin Seasoltz describes the
new rite:

"The primary criterion that guided the preparation of
the new order was that of simplification of the ceremonial development undergone through the ages by
the old rituals of dedication. Chapters two, three, and
four, containing the rites for the dedication of a church
and altar, are the most important chapters in the document. The new rituals for these occasions, replacing
rites that date from 1294 and that were partially reformed in 1961, eliminate many duplications in words

114

and gestures, so that what used to be a very long celebration is now lengthy but considerably shortened."[41]

Chapter 2 of the new rite deals with the dedication of a church. The rite, which ordinarily should be performed by the local bishop [6], takes place in the context of the eucharist; indeed, "the celebration of the eucharist is the most important rite, and the only necessary one, for the dedication of a church" [15]. In the early centuries, a church was dedicated simply by the eucharist being celebrated there for the first time. While the *lustratio* of the new edifice was added in the liturgy of Rome from at least the sixth century on, it was the Gallican liturgy that created an extremely complex ceremony.[42] The famous parallel construct began in Gaul: just as the individual Christian becomes the temple of God by receiving in succession the sacraments of baptism, confirmation, and eucharist, so the edifice becomes a temple of God by lustral ablutions (baptism), anointing with sacred oils (confirmation), and the celebration of the eucharist.[43]

In the new rite the *lustratio* is less a purification than a reminder of a previous baptism: "Bless this water; sanctify it. As it is sprinkled upon us and throughout this church make it a sign of the saving waters of baptism, by which we become one in Christ, the temple of your Spirit" [48]. The dedication and anointings take place after the liturgy of the word. The prayer of dedication contains an invocation of the Spirit: "Lord, send your Spirit from heaven to make this church an ever-holy place, and this altar a ready table for the sacrifice of Christ" [62]. In the past there had been two separate consecratory prayers: one for the church and one for the altar. The new rite shows the underlying unity between church and altar by providing one single prayer. This single prayer of dedication is followed by the anointings of the altar and church walls. Traditionally the altar has been the symbol of Christ (the Anointed One), and the walls (or church stones) symbolize Christ's members. Calabuig says:

"If in the building dedicated to worship the altar is Christ, the stones holding up the walls are Christians (see I Peter 2:5). As the Head was anointed with the Spirit, so are the members in the sacraments; as the altar was anointed, so are the stones. The anointing of the new church's inner walls appears as ritual translation of this relationship, and as a second stage in the Christian initiation of the new ecclesial space."[44]

The bishop first anoints the altar with chrism. Only he, the "high priest of the flock," does this, but he may invite his priests to concelebrate with him in anointing the church walls. The anointing of the altar should not be stingy: "It is recommended that he anoint the entire table of the altar with chrism" [64]. The anointing aspect of the rite is powerful. First the altar is anointed, the symbol of Christ, the Anointed One; then the walls, the symbol of his anointed people. The church edifice will thus stand as a symbol of the unity of Christ with his people.

Chapter Seven treats of the blessing of a chalice and paten. The former practice of consecrating chalices with chrism has been dropped. Now chalices and patens are merely blessed, and even that would seem to be optional. What would best bless such an object would be its being used in the liturgy.

The new rite makes no provision for the blessing of church bells. Down through the centuries we find church bells being blessed, sometimes with chrism, sometimes with the oil of catechumens, and sometimes even with the oil of the sick. It is unfortunate that the new rite does not include a blessing of church bells, as in some places, especially in rural areas, they still play an important role in calling people to worship.

116

Another use of oil and chrism that has been discontinued in the modern liturgical reform is in the blessing of baptismal water. Formerly during the Easter Vigil, chrism and the oil of catechumens were added to the baptismal water. The practice of putting chrism into the water was Gallican in origin, apparently deriving from the East, which entered the Roman liturgy through the Gelasian usage of the eighth century but was not taken up in all areas of the Roman rite until the Roman Missal of Pius V in 1570.[45] The oldest sources mention only chrism. Since the tenth century the oil of catechumens was also used. Placing chrism in the baptismal water symbolized the Holy Spirit's coming down on the waters at the dawn of creation, as well as the connotation that the bishop was involved here, since he was the one who had consecrated the chrism in the first place.[46] The action of blessing the baptismal water with oil, therefore, had a pneumatic orientation. The Holy Spirit was to come down on this water just as he had descended upon the waters at the dawn of creation.

The present liturgy of the Easter Vigil totally omits putting oil and chrism into the water. This omission is not surprising, since the Roman mentality, as opposed to the Eastern and the Gallican, never viewed the mixing of chrism in the baptismal water as the constitutive element; it was the prayer itself. In the new liturgy of the Easter Vigil the celebrant blesses the water, lowering the Easter candle into the water as he says, "We ask you, Father, with your Son to send the Holy Spirit upon the waters of this font." Holding the candle in the water he continues, "May all who are buried with Christ in the death of baptism rise also with him to newness of life. We ask this through Christ our Lord. Amen." The action of lowering the Easter candle into the water and then raising it out again is christocentric in orientation, symbolizing his death and resurrection.

Yet, this christocentric ritual has an artificial trinitarian formula imposed on it: "We ask you, Father, with your Son to send the Holy Spirit upon the water of this font."

CONCLUSION

A number of uses of oil and chrism have dropped out of practice during the centuries. One wonders if a cause of this discontinuation was the way the oils were used so minimally in the sacramental rites themselves. If oils were dabbed on sparingly with a thumb and then quickly rubbed off with cotton, the people participating in the rite would scarcely be challenged to conjure up in their imaginations all the qualities and powers of oil with which they were familiar in their daily lives. This consideration is important for our usages of oil and chrism today. The sign must not be veiled, but must be used in all its vigor.

The prebaptismal anointing is performed on the breast (or on both hands or on other parts of the body for adults) with the oil of catechumens.[47] The postbaptismal anointing is done on the crown of the head, and the confirmation anointing is on the forehead. Both are done with chrism. A church is dedicated by anointing its altar and walls with chrism. The meaning of these actions begins with the basic understanding that Christians have of oil and chrism. Certainly oils and perfumes play an important role in modern life: they soothe, heal, strengthen, protect, cleanse, warm, and exhilarate. These meanings will be amplified when placed in the context of Christians' sharing in the life of "the anointed one," Jesus Christ. By initiation Christians are plunged into the paschal mystery of Christ; they, like Christ, are anointed with the Spirit. This mystery gradually unfolds itself in the symbol life of the Christian community as oil and chrism are used in a context of belief.

118

NOTES

1. *Ordo Benedicendi Oleum Catechumenorum et Infirmorum et Conficiendi Chrisma* (Typis Polyglottis Vaticanis, Vatican City 1971). See *The Rites of the Catholic Church* (Pueblo, New York 1976), pp. 515–527 (or *The Rites of the Catholic Church*, vol. 2, pp. 302–312), which follows the English translation of *Rite of Confirmation, Rite of the Blessing of Oils, Rite of Consecrating the Chrism*, ICEL 1972.

2. *Notitiae* 7 (1971), pp. 89–92.

3. The oil of the sick will not be treated here in any length, since this discussion is included in Charles W. Gusmer, *And You Visited Me: Sacramental Ministry to the Sick and the Dying* (Pueblo, New York 1984), vol. 6 of the series, *Studies in the Reformed Rites of the Catholic Church.*

4. See chapter 2, "Origins of Baptismal Anointing" in Leonel L. Mitchell, *Baptismal Anointing* (SPCK, London 1966), pp. 10–29. Also, see Philipp Hofmeister, *Die Heiligen Öle in der Morgen- und Abendländischen Kirche* (Augustinus-Verlag, Würzburg 1948), pp. 18–125. Also, J. Ysebaert, *Greek Baptismal Terminology: Its Origins and Early Development* (Dekker & Van De Vegt, Nijmegen 1962), pp. 182–426.

5. Mitchell, p. 28.

6. Raymond E. Brown, "We Profess One Baptism for the Forgiveness of Sins," *Worship* 40 (1966), p. 264.

7. Ernest Evans (ed.), *Tertullian's Homily on Baptism* (SPCK, London 1964), p. 17.

8. See Bernard Botte (ed.), *La Tradition Apostolique de Saint Hippolyte* (Aschendorff, Münster 1963). For the convenience of the reader, the references in Whitaker will also be given: E. C. Whitaker (ed.), *Documents of the Baptismal Liturgy* (SPCK, London 1970).

9. Botte, p. 47; Whitaker, p. 5.

10. Ibid.

11. Botte, p. 51; Whitaker, p. 6.

12. Botte, p. 53; Whitaker, p. 6.

13. In the Syrian Orthodox churches, the bishop blessed the oils on Holy Thursday up until the thirteenth century. In the Armenian churches, the blessing was reserved to the Catholicos already by the eighth century.

14. F. L. Cross (ed.), *St. Cyril of Jerusalem's Lectures on the Christian Sacraments* (SPCK, London 1960), p. 65.

15. Whitaker, p. 34.

16. For this section I am heavily indebted to two excellent articles: Pierre Jounel, "La consécration du chrême et la bénédiction des saintes huiles," *La Maison-Dieu* 112 (1972), pp. 70–83; Robert Beraudy, "Le saint chrême et l'onction postbaptismale" in A. G. Martimort (ed.), *L'Eglise en Prière* (Desclée, Paris 1965), pp. 557–561.

17. See G. Morin, "Une particularité arlésienne de la liturgie du samedi saint," *Ephemerides Liturgicae* 49 (1935), pp. 146–149.

18. See Michel Andrieu (ed.), *Les Ordines Romani du Haut Moyen-Age* III (Spicilegium Sacrum Lovaniense, Louvain 1961), pp. 269–270.

19. See Antoine Chavasse, *Le sacramentaire gélasien* (Desclée, Paris 1958), pp. 137–139.

20. L. C. Mohlberg (ed.), *Liber Sacramentorum Romanae Aeclesiae Ordinis Anni Circuli* (Herder, Rome 1960), pp. 60–63.

21. For the history of the Gelasian chrism formula, see Chavasse, pp. 133–139.

22. Cyrille Vogel (ed.), *Le Pontifical Romano-Germanique du Dixième Siècle* II (Biblioteca Apostolica Vaticana, Vatican City 1963), pp. 71–75.

23. Ibid., p. 72.

24. Michel Andrieu (ed.), *Le Pontifical Romain au moyen-age* III: *Le Pontifical de Guillaume Durand* (Biblioteca Apostolica Vaticana, Vatican City 1940), pp. 573–579.

25. For a listing of such conciliar legislation, see Eugene M. Finnegan, "The Origins of Confirmation in the Western Church: A Liturgical-Dogmatic Study of the Development of

the Separate Sacrament of Confirmation in the Western Church Prior to the Fourteenth Century," unpublished doctoral thesis; Theological Faculty of Trier, Germany, 1970, pp. 424–425.

26. This confusion dates all the way back to the third century. See Botte, *La Tradition Apostolique*, pp. 18–19. For more precise nuances see E. Segelberg, "The Benedictio Olei in the Apostolic Tradition of Hippolytus," *Oriens Christianus* 48 (1964), pp. 268–281.

27. See also *Rite of Christian Initiation of Adults*, nos. 206 and 218.

28. Cross, p. 60.

29. Hugh M. Riley, *Christian Initiation* (Catholic University of America Press, Washington, D.C. 1974), pp. 189–211.

30. Gabriele Winkler, *Das Armenische Initiationsrituale*, (Orientalia Christiana Analecta 217 (Pont. Institutum Studiorum Orientalium, Rome 1982), pp. 401–422.

31. It is found, substantially, in the Gelasian Sacramentary: L. C. Mohlberg (ed.), p. 62.

32. For an excellent commentary on the consecratory prayer, see Jean Rogues, "La préface consécratoire du chrême," *La Maison-Dieu* 49 (1957), pp. 35–49.

33. See Ignace de la Potterie, " 'To Be Born Again of Water and the Spirit': The Baptismal Text of John 3:5" in *The Christian Lives by the Spirit* (Alba House, Staten Island, N.Y. 1971), pp. 1–36.

34. L. C. Mohlberg (ed.), pp. 55–64.

35. *Revised Rites of Holy Week*, Holy Thursday: Evening Mass of the Lord's Supper, no. 5.

36. See Niels Rasmussen, "The Chrism Mass: Tradition and Renewal" in *The Cathedral: A Reader* (USCC Publications, Washington, D.C. 1979), pp. 29–33.

37. Raymond E. Brown, "The Challenge of the Three Biblical Priesthoods," *Catholic Mind* 78 (1980), p. 15.

38. J. Frank Henderson, "The Chrism Mass of Holy Thursday," *Worship* 51 (1977), p. 150.

39. *Sacrosanctum Concilium* 33 (*Documents on the Liturgy*, no. 33).

40. See *The Rites*, vol. 2, pp. 185–293.

41. R. Kevin Seasoltz, *New Liturgy, New Laws* (Liturgical Press, Collegeville, Minn. 1980), p. 130.

42. The oldest Gallican order of dedication is in the Sacramentary of Angoulême: P. Cagin (ed.), *Le Sacramentaire gélasien d'Angoulême* (Edition diplomatique, Angoulême 1918), p. 140.

43. See Ignazio M. Calabuig, *The Dedication of a Church and an Altar: A Theological Commentary* (U.S. Catholic Conference, Washington, D.C. 1980), p. 12.

44. Ibid., p. 26.

45. See L. C. Mohlberg (ed.), *Missale Gothicum* (Herder, Rome 1961), p. 67. See also E. Lengeling, "Blessing of Baptismal Water in the Roman Rite" in J. Wagner (ed.), *Adult Baptism and the Catechumenate*, Concilium 22 (Paulist Press, New York 1967), pp. 62–68.

46. See R. Béraudy, "Initiation chrétienne" in A. G. Martimort (ed.), *L'Eglise en Prière* (Desclée, Paris 1965), pp. 553–554.

47. The U.S. bishops determined, "The prebaptismal anointing with the oil of catechumens may be omitted when the minister of baptism judges the omission to be pastorally necessary or desirable." *Newsletter: Bishops' Committee on the Liturgy* 5 (1969) no. 12.

The Future

Chapter Six

Observations and Guidelines

To survey the present situation of sacramental initiatory practice in the Roman Catholic Church is to become quickly dismayed. The vast majority are baptized as infants; their next sacramental preparation is for first penance and first eucharist; some years later they are confirmed. In other words, in midstream, before the initiation process is even completed, the movement toward full initiation is disrupted and young Christians are reinitiated by first penance.[1] The issue is next complicated by giving first communion to those whose baptisms have not yet been sealed in confirmation. Such a situation is theologically chaotic and pastorally unmanageable. There is, then, no solution to the confirmation question independent of this larger picture.

INFANT BAPTISM
The first element of this larger picture is the question of infant baptism. Can the practice be questioned seriously? Should it be continued?

Whether infants were baptized in the New Testament decades is a disputed point.[2] Raymond Brown says:

"The most that can be asserted is that such baptism of children was acceptable; there is no real evidence that the baptism of children and infants was thought necessary. . . . Where children were baptized, the apparent reason is to bring a whole family into the church—a sense of solidarity. There is no clear evidence that infants were baptized to remove original sin. Indeed, the whole problem of original sin in the Augustinian sense does not seem to enter into New Testament baptismal thought."[3]

The basic focus and concern of the primitive church was the conversion and baptism of adults. Because they had sinned in their personal lives, adults had need of conversion and the ritual expression of that conversion was baptism.

It was only after the sixth century, when adult baptism had become a rarity, that full attention was turned to the baptism of infants. For Augustine, the fact that the church baptized infants was a proof of the universality of original sin. He was not arguing that infants should be baptized because they possessed original sin, but rather that *de facto* they must be in sin since the church baptizes them.[4] It was only in the ninth century with Walafrid Strabo that the existence of original sin became the justification for infant baptism.[5] During the Middle Ages the increasing stress on the fact of original sin, along with a high rate of infant mortality, led to an insistence on infant baptism. It was generally believed that infants who died unbaptized could not enjoy the blessings of eternal life. St. Bernard of Clairvaux (d. 1153), for example, wrote that when the grace of baptism is denied to them, infants of Christians do not attain the life of Christ, and the way to salvation is closed to them.[6] Thus, a rethinking of the practice of infant baptism is necessarily tied in to a rethinking of the theology of original sin.[7]

While the commission responsible for drawing up the 1969 *Rite of Baptism for Children* never even considered dropping the practice of infant baptism, many theologians today are considering alternate approaches. In December 1973, seventy-five American liturgists, representing several Christian churches, convened in Scottsdale, Arizona, to celebrate the tenth anniversary of the *Constitution on the Sacred Liturgy* of Vatican II. Their statement on Christian initiation includes the following remark: "For children of responsible Christian parents, two different patterns of initiation might well coexist: the celebration of the full rite of initiation (baptism, confirmation, Eucharist) shortly after birth, to be followed by catechesis appropriate to succeeding stages of development; or enrollment of the infant as a catechumen, with initiation to be celebrated at a later age after catechesis."[8] This latter pattern is favored by many theologians as being more pastorally advantageous.[9] It would seem, however, that there are problems with this point of view. If the parents are truly committed Christians, is there any real advantage in not baptizing the children in infancy? In such cases it would seem that infant baptism would signify both the notion of the solidarity of the believing family and the fact that it is God who takes the initiative. There is one case, perhaps, where first enrolling the infant in the catechumenate could prove extremely helpful—namely, when the parents request baptism for their child but do not show adequate indication that the child would be raised in an atmosphere of faith. Some would say there is a parallel here with marriages that are not fully mature Christian unions, so a simple "blessing" might be given to maintain a connection with the church until such time as the faith commitment of the couple would warrant a sacramental marriage in the church.

As to delaying baptism, the U.S. Bishops' Committee on the Liturgy states: "When there is no possibility that a child will enjoy a Christian environment and example, and no reasonable hope that the faith to be shared with a child will survive, baptism should be delayed, until such time as reasonable hope does exist, except in danger of death."[10]

Where infant baptism is *de facto* celebrated, one can
well ask: Why not also celebrate confirmation and first
eucharist at this point? If there is adequate reason for
not delaying baptism is there not also reason for not
delaying the completion of initiation? Why should a
certain knowledge of what one is doing be required for
confirmation and eucharist, but not for baptism? The
Eastern practice of complete initiation in infancy not
only keeps intact the sacraments of initiation, but it
symbolizes that God's gratuitous love is operative. "In
this is love, not that we loved God but that he loved
us and sent his Son to be the expiation for our sins"
(1 Jn 4:10).

Our present separation of the three sacraments of initiation is more than just a departure from the early
liturgical tradition. It is a theological impoverishment.
Eucharist must not be viewed merely as the transubstantiation of the elements; it is the fulfillment of baptism, and leads to the actualization of the church. Alexander Schmemann puts it well:

"Clearly only such understanding and experience of the
Eucharist reveals it as the self-evident and necessary
fulfillment of Baptism. Baptism, we are told, *integrates*
us into the Church. But if the Church's ultimate being
and essence are revealed in and through the Eucharist,
if Eucharist is truly *the sacrament of the Church* and not
only one of the Church's sacraments, then of necessity
to enter the Church is to enter into the Eucharist, then
Eucharist is indeed the fulfillment of Baptism."[11]

He would, of course, place chrismation between the
two: "If Chrismation, as we have tried to show, fulfills
Baptism, Eucharist is the fulfillment of Chrismation.
. . . In Baptism we are born again of Water and the
Spirit, and it is this birth which makes us *open* to the
gift of the Holy Spirit, to our personal Pentecost. And

finally, it is the gift of the Holy Spirit that 'opens' to us access to the Church, to Christ's table in His Kingdom.''[12]

The 1969 *Rite of Baptism for Children* retained the anointing with chrism immediately following the water-bath, but changed the accompanying prayer to highlight more clearly the royal priesthood of the baptized. Formerly the following formula accompanied the anointing on the crown of the head with chrism: "The almighty God, Father of our Lord Jesus Christ, has caused you to be born over again of water and the Holy Spirit and pardoned you all your sins. May He now anoint you with the chrism that sanctifies in Christ Jesus our Lord, and bring you to everlasting life.''[13] In the new rite the prayer is said, and then the anointing is done in silence. The new formula is: "God the Father of our Lord Jesus Christ has freed you from sin, given you a new birth by water and the Holy Spirit, and welcomed you into his holy people. He now anoints you with the chrism of salvation. As Christ was anointed Priest, Prophet, and King, so may you live always as members of his body, sharing everlasting life. Amen" [62]. While the new wording is a step forward, nevertheless, some liturgists thought the postbaptismal anointing should have been omitted. They cited the confusion caused in trying to distinguish this action from confirmation itself.[14] Thus, even the postbaptismal anointing found in the new *Rite of Infant Baptism* separates the three sacraments of initiation by not sufficiently relating baptism to confirmation and eucharist. If complete initiation of infants were to be reinstated in the West, the postbaptismal anointing should be dropped, just as it has been dropped in the case of older children and adults in the new *Rite of Christian Initiation of Adults* [35] [224].

The practice of communicating infants as part of initiation existed in the West until around the thirteenth century.[15] In the early church, baptism and eucharist were inseparable. The two commands of Christ were seen as one reality: "Truly, truly, I say to you, unless one is born of water and the Spirit, he cannot enter the kingdom of God" (Jn 3:5), and "Truly, truly, I say to you, unless you eat the flesh of the Son of man and drink his blood, you have no life in you" (Jn 6:53). This attitude lasted until the practice of communicating newly baptized infants began to cease. The reason for the change is complex. David Holeton writes:

"To suggest that the practice began to disappear with the proclamation of transubstantiation and the withdrawal of the chalice from the laity is to miss the principal point. A Christian society that has degenerated to such a state that it becomes necessary to legislate that Christians need receive the eucharist once a year is fertile for most everything to take place in the context of baptism and the eucharist. The whole vision of what the eucharist was, and what its relationship was to the community, had so changed that the process could take place unresisted, except in those places where tradition was being asserted for political rather than theological reasons."[16]

The practice of infant communion was officially abolished by the Council of Trent when it was stated that baptized children who do not yet have the use of reason are not under any obligation to receive the eucharist, since at their age they cannot lose the grace of the children of God that they received in their baptism.[17] Trent did not say it was wrong to communicate infants. How could it in the light of Eastern practice, and even Western practice for hundreds of years? The 1917 Code of Canon Law regulated that the eucharist would not be administered to children who, because of the deficiency of age, do not have the knowledge or the intention required for the reception of this sacrament.[18]

One wonders if this shift in sacramental practice toward not communicating infants and young children indicates an impoverished sacramental understanding. Certainly there is no theological reason for withholding the eucharist from baptized infants, assuming they are not indiscriminately baptized. The judgment should not be made on the level of the individual alone, but must, like infant baptism, be seen in a familial and ecclesial context. The value involved is one that comes out of a believing community, where a child grows normally into the faith-life of its parents, sharing the food of the altar with its parents over a period of years.[19] It is similar to the child who hears good music played in the home right from the beginning; the growth in appreciation of the music is almost imperceptible. The title for admission to the Table of the Lord is far clearer through the sacraments of baptism and confirmation than through something as undetermined and nebulous as the age of discretion.

FIRST CONFESSION

First confession before first communion interrupts the initiation process for many in the present sacramental practice. A great deal has been written about this matter,[20] and much of the debate at the moment centers around how one interprets the 1910 decree of the Sacred Congregation of the Sacraments, *Quam Singulari*.[21] Some suggest having penitential services for young children with general absolution.[22] The *National Catechetical Directory for Catholics of the United States* seems to have reached a way of handling the problem by stating: "The Sacrament of Reconciliation normally should be celebrated prior to the reception of First Communion."[23] Thus, there is an increasing practice of having a penitential service for first communicants and their parents some time before first communion, where optional private confession would be available for those who want it. Still the catechetical problem remains: how to prepare young children for the two diverse sacraments of penance and eucharist at the same time so that one does not detract from the other, and so that the children will not always put the two sacraments together in their minds in the future.

Penance interrupts the initiation process because essentially the sacrament is a reinitiation, a reestablishment of the original unity created by the initiation sacraments of baptism, confirmation, and eucharist. Aidan Kavanagh puts it well:

"The sacramental stages comprising Christian initiation (baptism, confirmation, and Eucharist) must be seen in context of the paschal mystery. All these find their liturgical elaboration first within the period of the paschal season, forming the fabric of the Easter vigil celebration from the earliest times. In this perspective penance is revealed *au fond* as a close sacramental analogue of the initiation complex: it is a celebration of metanoia, or reinitiation into the converting community, a re-establishment of union with him who alone has power to forgive sins in his body the Church. Thus baptism and penance are closely allied. In this the two are the same, that each establishes union with the *totus Christus,* Christ in his Church. In this the two differ, that the one realizes the union in an initial manner while the other reactualizes the union once this has been sundered by sin. Each attains their proper fulness of union in Christ in the Eucharist, the *res* or ultimate purpose of which is the unity of the body of Christ."[24]

If one remembers this important theological dimension, one finds it difficult to justify the practice of placing the first confession of children before their first communion. The practice presupposes that the initial unity with Christ created in baptism has been sundered by serious sin. In the case of young children this can hardly be the case. Finally, when contrasting first penance and confirmation in the present pastoral practice, it can be asked if far more is not being demanded for the reception of confirmation than for the reception of first penance. Maturity and commitment are demanded of those receiving confirmation, while far less seems to suffice for the reception of first penance.

FIRST COMMUNION

In modern times first communion was usually deferred until the ages of ten to fourteen. In 1910, Pope Pius X lowered that age in the decree *Quam Singulari*: "The age of discretion for receiving Holy Communion is that at which the child knows the difference between the Eucharistic Bread and ordinary, material bread, and can therefore approach the altar with proper devotion."[25] While this reform brought reception of the eucharist to young children, in most places throughout the world the age for the reception of confirmation was not correspondingly lowered. This was another contribution, then, to the separation of confirmation from eucharist at the same time that it tended to identify the age of first communion with that of first penance: "The age of discretion, both for Confession and for Holy Communion, is the time when a child begins to reason, that is about the seventh year, more or less. From that time on begins the obligation of fulfilling the precept of both Confession and Communion."[26] As to catechetical preparation for first communion, the decree is not overly demanding: "Perfect knowledge of the things of faith, therefore, is not required, for an elementary knowledge suffices—some knowledge (*aliqua cognitio*); similarly full use of reason is not required, for a certain beginning of the use of reason, that is, some use of reason (*aliqualis usus rationis*) suffices. To postpone Communion, therefore, until later and to insist on a more mature age for its reception must be absolutely discouraged."[27] Curiously, in this entire discussion the sacrament of confirmation is never mentioned.

133

Further insights into the relationship between the three sacraments of baptism, confirmation, and eucharist may be gleaned by viewing the various types and forms of commitment necessary in living out the Christian life. One aspect of the problem is seen in the unrepeatability of confirmation. Confirmation is essentially tied in with a once-and-for-all incorporation into the Body of Christ; the gift, the Spirit, is given that one may realize that Body in the world. While the incorporation takes place only once, the expression and completion of this reality happens time and again in the day-in and day-out life of the Christian. The "Statement on Christian Commitment" by the Bishops' Committee on the Liturgy says: "Christian initiation, while happening once and for all through the initial participation in the paschal mystery of Jesus, must also be a moment-to-moment process of saying yes to the Lord at each step in life's pilgrimage."[28]

So it is that there is need for many and varied ways in the life of the church to show signs of Christian commitment. Confirmation must not be expected to bear the entire burden. The liturgical year provides excellent opportunities, especially the annual celebration of the Easter Vigil with its renewal of the vows of baptism. There are such things as the sacrament of penance, the days of Lent, and moments of personal decision. Moments of personal decision would include not only general decisions to persevere in God's grace, but such concrete decisions as to take marriage vows or vows of religion, or various ordained (or nonordained) ministries in the life of the church. "All these special moments along the path of life demand decisions rooted in a christian life of committed faith."[29] Above all there is the eucharist. "At each celebration of the eucharist the christian is challenged to renew his commitment to the Gospel of Jesus Christ, to membership in his body, the

Church, and to the living of the covenanted relationship with the Lord manifested by a life of service to others. As such, the eucharist is the repeatable sacrament of initiation."[30] The eucharist is the way *par excellence* that Christians celebrate the paschal mystery in their lives. The eucharist makes the sacrifice of Christ the sacrifice of the church, and each time it is celebrated one should commit oneself more completely. One should grow into this as normally and logically as one grows into physical and psychic maturity.

The various ways of renewing Christian commitment have been neglected in Roman Catholic life. For many, confirmation was supposed to bear the weight of "committing oneself to the Lord." Yet, deep down there has been a dissatisfaction with this thinking. At the root of the difficulty has been an attempt to identify the different sacraments of initiation with distinct moments in the life cycle. Confirmation was thus seen as the passage into maturity.[31] Stevick says: "It is psychologically self-defeating to try to associate one part of the initiatory unity with one stage of life, and other parts with other stages when no such staged-out meanings belong inherently to the rites themselves."[32]

The fact that some sacramental theologians identify the initiation sacraments with distinct moments in the life cycle while others do not has given rise to two schools of thought. Those who deny the identification tend to stress aspects of dogmatic and liturgical theology and argue for the unity of the initiation process and the traditional order of baptism, confirmation, and eucharist. Those who affirm the identification of the initiation sacraments with the moments in the life cycle tend to stress pastoral and anthropological aspects of theology and argue for the faith involvement of the subject, viewed from the psychological explanation of the development of personality. They would not insist on the traditional ordering of the sacraments and would argue for a later age of confirmation at the time of adolescence—just how late depending on such things as various theories of moral development.

A problem identified with this second school of thought (those who would delay confirmation to a later age) comes from the very notion of adolescence. The concept as such is a relatively new one. Joseph Kett, a noted social historian, writes:

"Between 1890 and 1920 a host of psychologists, urban reformers, educators, youth workers, and parent counselors gave shape to the concept of adolescence, leading to the massive reclassification of young people as adolescents. . . . To speak of the 'invention of the adolescent' rather than of the discovery of adolescence underscores a related point: adolescence was essentially a conception of behavior imposed on youth, rather than an empirical assessment of the way in which young people actually behaved."[33]

It would seem imperative to guard against building a theology of confirmation on such a relative and elusive concept as adolescence.

CONFIRMATION IN THE CONTEXT
OF THE INITIATION PROCESS

There is no solution to such undivided opinion as long as confirmation is viewed only on its own terms. The context of confirmation must be the broader vision of the initiation sacraments. In other words, the mandate of the *Constitution on the Sacred Liturgy* must be taken seriously: "The rite of confirmation is to be revised in order that the intimate connection of this sacrament with the whole of Christian initiation may stand out more clearly."[34] Furthermore, the theological norm for understanding confirmation is the initiation of adults, not of infants. There is a parallel here with baptism: one does not theologize about baptism using infant baptism as the norm. In this vein it would have been more logical to have the commission that produced the new rites of baptism also produce the *Rite of Confirmation*. But Bernard Botte, a member of the confirmation commission, says no one even thought of it.[35]

The intimate connection between baptism and confirmation is brought out well by the *Rite of Christian Initiation of Adults:*

"According to the ancient practice maintained in the Roman liturgy, an adult is not to be baptized unless he receives confirmation immediately afterward, provided no serious obstacles exist. This connection signifies the unity of the paschal mystery, the close relationship (*necessitudo*) between the mission of the Son and the pouring out of the Holy Spirit, and the joint celebration of the sacraments by which the Son and the Spirit come with the Father upon those who are baptized" [34].

Does not this statement directly challenge from a theological point of view our present pastoral practice? How can this connection be taken seriously for adults, but totally ignored for infants and young children? Confirmation has been so disconnected from baptism that both sacraments have become the poorer: baptism is seen only in a negative sense as forgiveness of sins, and confirmation is reduced to a mere ratification of a previous baptism.

The same point is brought out by the liturgy of the *Rite of Baptism for Children*. At the conclusion of the rite there is a procession to the altar, a strong symbol that initiation reaches its apex only in the eucharist. The celebrant admits that what has been done is only a beginning: "Dearly beloved, these children have been reborn in baptism. They are now called children of God, for so indeed they are. In confirmation they will receive the fullness of God's Spirit. In holy communion

they will share the banquet of Christ's sacrifice, calling God their Father in the midst of the Church" [68].
Time and again the liturgy witnesses to the intimate relationship between the three sacraments of initiation. Confirmation must be seen in this context. Baptism brings incorporation into Christ. The baptized are called to receive on the level of gift that which Christ has by nature: the Holy Spirit, who at the Jordan revealed Jesus as the Anointed.[36] The baptized are called to receive not only the gifts of the Spirit, but the Spirit itself. The gift is the Spirit.

There is a great risk of diluting baptism if it is viewed only as accomplishing the forgiveness of sins and does not also involve the giving of the Holy Spirit. In the case of the disciples who experienced the Pentecost event, there was no need to receive the Christian sacrament of baptism. Yet as David Stanley points out:

"The same consciousness of the unique character of their own (Pentecostal) experience led them, according to the evidence of the New Testament (Acts 2:41), to impart Christian baptism to those who wished to be added 'to the number of the saved' (Acts 2:47). In fact, we may say that the apostles looked upon the reception of this sacrament as reproducing, so far as that was possible, their own Pentecostal experience."[37]

This type of thinking preserves the necessary connection between baptism and the Pentecost experience. It preserves the unity of the paschal mystery, as opposed to the thinking that equates baptism with the Easter mystery and confirmation with the Pentecost mystery. The same unity is underscored by the new formula of confirmation, "Be sealed with the Gift of the Holy Spirit." Modeled on the ancient Byzantine formula, it is based on Peter's preaching at Jerusalem: "Repent, and be baptized every one of you in the name of Jesus Christ for the forgiveness of your sins; and you shall receive the gift of the Holy Spirit" (Acts 2:38). Christ's death and resurrection cannot be separated just as forgiveness of sins cannot be separated from the bestowal of the Spirit. "Do you not know that all of us who have been baptized into Christ Jesus were baptized into his death? We were buried therefore with him by baptism into death, so that as Christ was raised from the dead by the glory of the Father, we too might walk in newness of life" (Rom 6:3–4). This walking in newness of life is no other than the "walking by the Spirit" of Galatians 5:16.

Baptism and confirmation are both, in their turn, further ordered to the eucharist. The *Rite of Confirmation* states: "Ordinarily confirmation takes place within Mass in order to express more clearly the fundamental connection of this sacrament with the entirety of Christian initiation. The latter reaches its culmination in the communion of the body and blood of Christ. The newly confirmed should therefore participate in the eucharist which completes their Christian initiation" [13]. The *Rite of Christian Initiation of Adults* describes the completion of the sacraments of initiation: "Finally the eucharist is celebrated and for the first time the neophytes have the full right to take part. This is the culminating point of their initiation . . . by receiving the body that was handed over and the blood that was shed, they confirm the gifts they have received and acquire a foretaste of eternal things" [36]. It is interesting that the word "confirm" is used here. It corresponds to an ancient usage of the word signifying the completion of baptism and confirmation, by bringing initiation to its climax in the eucharist.[38] The Eastern churches have been faithful to this important concept of the eucharist as the apex of initiation, but the West has not.[39] Adrien Nocent writes of the importance of placing confirmation before first eucharist: "With Confirmation, we share more perfectly in the Eucharist. It is not that the

Eucharist itself undergoes change, but that we who receive and share it do so from now on in a new quality and with a greater conformity to Christ who working through his mystery is made present."[40]

The strongest argument for the interrelationship of baptism, confirmation, and eucharist comes from an analysis of the structure of confirmation itself. Aidan Kavanagh argues that

"consignation-confirmation, something unique and peculiar to the Roman out of all other rites, seems to be, in terms of structural analysis, the distinct yet inseparable *missa* synaxis which consummates baptism-chrismation on the one hand and sends the neophytes directly into eucharist on the other. . . . We suggest that all confirmation ever was or really has been is episcopal prayer over neophytes and their coming to the bishop's hand, where they are reminded solemnly of their chrismation by a second anointing and dismissed into their first eucharist."[41]

He warns that when confirmation is separated from the two mysteries of baptism and eucharist, confirmation's "character and function as *missa* is destroyed and anomalies in practice and interpretation then adversely affect the whole of sacramental initiation."[42]

This interrelationship of the initiation sacraments is most clearly seen in the context of adult initiation. When adults are baptized they are immediately confirmed (omitting the postbaptismal anointing) and given first eucharist. The right order of the initiation sacraments is thus guaranteed and expected. Also, the initiation process makes it clear that the Holy Spirit has been operative throughout. The catechumens embark on a spiritual journey that is guided and led by the Spirit. The *Rite of Christian Initiation of Adults* states that from the very time of the rite of becoming a catechumen, the catechumens "are joined to the

Church and are part of the household of Christ. . . .
One who dies during the catechumenate receives a
Christian burial" [18].

The fact that the Holy Spirit is operative in the lives of
the catechumens is ritualized during the catechumenate
in various ways, especially by the scrutinies. What is
crucial here is that the Spirit is operating in and
through the mediation of the Christian community.
The rite says: "The initiation of catechumens takes
place step by step in the midst of the community of
the faithful. Together with the catechumens, the
faithful reflect upon the value of the paschal mystery,
renew their own conversion, and by their example
lead the catechumens to obey the Holy Spirit more
generously" [4]. This process might take a long time,
sometimes even years, but that is not important; the
Spirit is already at work. In such a context it is clear
that the sacrament of confirmation does not celebrate
the first reception of the Holy Spirit in the lives of the
candidates, but is a publicly manifested crescendo in
a Spirit-filled journey.

GUIDELINES FOR A SOLUTION
In light of confirmation's complex historical development, we might well ask how the tangled knot of
present pastoral practice can be unraveled. In the context of all that has been said so far, I will attempt to set
forth seven guidelines toward a solution.

First, the theology of baptism must be viewed not only
under the aspect of dying (Rom 6), but under the
aspect of birth event (Jn 3) as well. In this regard the
richness of the Eastern tradition should be tapped. In
the East the baptismal liturgy, at least in its earliest
ritualization, kept its eyes on the Jordan event as the
prime analogue and expressed itself as birth event into
the eschatological reality. Gabriele Winkler writes of

the early Syrian liturgy that knew only a prebaptismal anointing:

"In the oldest Syriac documents, Christian baptism is shaped after Christ's baptism in the Jordan. As Jesus had received the anointing through the divine presence in the appearance of a dove, and was invested as the Messiah, so in Christian baptism every candidate is anointed and, in connection with this anointing, the gift of the Spirit is conferred. Therefore the main theme of this pre-baptismal anointing is the entry into the eschatological kingship of the Messiah, being in the true sense of the word assimilated to the Messiah-King through this anointing."[43]

This tradition both enriches baptismal theology and stresses the intimate relationship between baptism and confirmation. The fact that the anointing precedes the water-bath highlights the oneness of the water-Spirit event.

Second, renewal in initiatory practices presupposes a rethinking of the fate of unbaptized children. While theologians today generally reject any notion of limbo as in no way demonstrable from the New Testament and as contradictory to the general divine will of redemption, nevertheless, this thinking has yet to trickle down to the popular level. Catechesis and preaching must face up to this problem.

Third, it is more important to preserve the unity of the paschal mystery symbolized by the initiation sacraments than to insist on the physical presence of a bishop at confirmation. Massey Shepherd writes:

"Much scholarly debate—centered always from our modern questions and problems—has been directed to analysing this paschal mystery—whether the fathers of the early church considered it one single rite or a complex of several successive sacramental acts, in

142

which we can distinguish our later separations in the Western Church of baptism, confirmation, and eucharist. But the fathers were not given to the niceties of scholastic distinctions. . . . They used the term 'baptism' indiscriminately to describe either the whole initiatory rite or one single aspect of it. They did not enumerate the sacraments (as did Peter Lombard) according to their specific form and matter. There was only one sacrament—the paschal mystery. It was a once-for-all act of incorporation into Christ, imparting forgiveness of sins, empowerment by the indwelling Holy Spirit, and an earnest of the kingdom of heaven."[44]

The East has preserved the presence of the bishop at confirmation by the insistence that he bless the chrism and thus be vicariously present in the chrism used. The West, on the other hand, has sacrificed the unity of the paschal mystery to hang on to the presence of the bishop. It is physically impossible for the bishop to be present at all baptisms. It must be asked—has not a higher value been sacrificed to maintain a lesser one?

Fourth, both theory and practice concerning confirmation must begin by the firm conviction that the two premier sacraments are baptism and eucharist. This was so in New Testament times; it is still so today. Baptism incorporates one into the Body of Christ, and eucharist builds up the unity of that Body. These two sacraments of baptism and eucharist mold all life in the church and determine the roles of the other sacraments. The sacrament of confirmation must not be an exception to this. Presently, the church pays more attention to confirmation than to baptism, and more is demanded by way of preparation for confirmation than for eucharist. We have forgotten the important statement of Thomas Aquinas, "The eucharist is the summit of the spiritual life, and the goal of all the sacraments."[45]

Fifth, any discussion of the character of confirmation as grounds for its unrepeatability must not be limited to a personal, individual level, but must be placed within an ecclesial context. This is true for all three sacraments that involve sacramental character: baptism, confirmation, and order.[46] Character is rooted not just in the branding or marking of an individual, but in a relationship between the recipient and Christ in which it is established that the church, the Body of Christ, might come into existence, and continue in existence. The unrepeatability of confirmation must be viewed in this context of ecclesiology; it is part of the once-and-for-all rite of becoming a Christian.

Sixth, confirmation should not be analyzed in its relation to baptism under the sole viewpoint of infant baptism, any more than one theologizes about baptism itself using infant baptism as the norm. A key question must be asked—are we using confirmation to make up for the deficiencies of infant baptism, which one scholar calls "a deficient form of baptism, a borderline version of the classical model of baptism"?[47] This does not mean that we should stop baptizing infants, but that we should stop the indiscriminate baptism of infants and intelligently consider, at least in certain cases, such options as enrolling infants in the catechumenate with appropriate catechesis and baptism and confirmation at a later age.

Seventh, when infants of committed Christian parents *are* baptized it would seem that all the sacraments of initiation should be given at that time, that is, the infants should be baptized, confirmed, and given first eucharist—as was done for over a thousand years in many places in the West and as is still done in the East. This approach would respect the traditional order of the sacraments of initiation: baptism, confirmation, eucharist. Such a practice would, of course, demand a change in the law as to who can confirm. If it were argued that this modification would lessen the contacts that a bishop has with his people, it should be honestly asked if the present situation is not in reality keeping bishops from more profitable visitations with the parishes in their dioceses.

Such a practice would underscore the reality that God takes the initiative, that baptism-confirmation-eucharist form an essential unity, and that admission to eucharist is built on incorporation into Christ and not upon something extrinsic such as knowledge or age. If this path of total initiation at infancy is not followed, at least the children baptized in infancy should be confirmed *prior* to first eucharist. In such a case the ideal would be confirmation and first eucharist at one and the same time. Such an approach would not destroy programs of religious catechesis; rather it would base such programs on personal development and needs and would be ongoing, rather than coming to a halt after the reception of confirmation.

All other views, and there are many, fail to place confirmation where it truly belongs, as part of the initiation process. They fail to take seriously the mandate of the *Constitution on the Sacred Liturgy:* "The rite of confirmation is to be revised and the intimate connection which this sacrament has with the whole of Christian initiation is to be more clearly set forth."[48] All other possibilities continue to place extraneous tasks on the shoulders of confirmation.

In the history of sacramental theology, we often meet a practice in search of a theory. Confirmation is a good example. J. D. C. Fisher writes:

"So in regard to confirmation we can say that for over a thousand years the Church in the West had been pleased to give confirmation to children of any age at their initiation, as the Eastern Church does to this day. But when because of practical difficulties and other causes, some of them deplorable causes, it came about that the majority of candidates for confirmation were not infants but adolescents, the Church in the West began to say, 'Infants are not now presented for confirmation: therefore infants do not need confirmation; the Church normally gives confirmation to adolescents: therefore the grace conveyed by confirmation must be the spiritual strength particularly needed by those entering adolescence'."[49]

The problem is that the new theory built upon confirmation practice, although concerned with important matters, ends up with something other than confirmation.[50] Confirmation is not a reaffirmation of a previous baptism; it is not the ritualization of a key moment in the human life cycle. It is, rather, the gift of the Spirit tied intimately to the water-bath that prepares one for the reception of the body and blood of Christ as a full member of the church.

NOTES

1. For the notion of penance as a reinitiation into the converting community see Aidan Kavanagh, "The Nature of Christian Penance: Metanoia and Reconciliation," *Resonance* 2 (1966), pp. 8–14.

2. For the debate see Karl Barth, *The Teaching of the Church Regarding Baptism* (SCM Press, London 1948); Oscar Cullmann, *Baptism in the New Testament* (SCM Press, London 1950); Joachim Jeremias, *Infant Baptism in the First Four Centuries* (Westminster Press, Philadelphia 1962); and Kurt Aland, *Did the Early Church Baptize Infants?* (Westminster Press, Philadelphia 1963). Barth and Aland take the negative side while Cullmann and Jeremias hold the positive.

3. Raymond Brown, "We Profess One Baptism for the Forgiveness of Sins," *Worship* 40 (1966), p. 265.

4. See J. C. Didier, "Saint Augustin et le baptême des enfants," *Revue des Etudes Augustiniennes* 2 (1956), pp. 109–129.

Some authors, however, would see the correlation between the practice of infant baptism and the doctrine of original sin taking place earlier. See, for example, Jaroslav Pelikan, *The Christian Tradition I: The Emergence of the Catholic Tradition (100–600)* (University of Chicago Press, Chicago 1971), pp. 290–292.

5. See J. C. Didier, *Faut-il baptiser les enfants? La réponse de la tradition* (Cerf, Paris 1967), pp. 208–209, 239–241.

6. Letter 241. Written in 1145.

7. For a helpful bibliographical overview of recent thinking on original sin see James L. Connor, "Original Sin: Contemporary Approaches," *Theological Studies* 29 (1968), pp. 215–240; Brian McDermott, "The Theology of Original Sin: Recent Developments," *Theological Studies* 38 (1977), pp. 478–512.

8. See John Gallen, "American Liturgy: A Theological Locus," *Theological Studies* 35 (1974), p. 307.

9. For example, Aidan Kavanagh, *The Shape of Baptism: The Rite of Christian Initiation* (Pueblo, New York 1978), p. 175.

10. *Newsletter: Bishops' Committee on the Liturgy* 14 (1978), p. 110.

11. Alexander Schmemann, *Of Water and the Spirit* (St. Vladimir's Seminary Press, New York 1974), pp. 117–118.

12. Ibid., p. 116.

13. Philip T. Weller (ed.), *The Roman Ritual* (Bruce, Milwaukee 1964), p. 59.

14. See Louis Ligier, "Le nouveau rituel du baptême des enfants," *La Maison-Dieu* 98 (1969), pp. 24–26.

15. See "The Separation of Communion from Initiation" in J. D. C. Fisher, *Christian Initiation: Baptism in the Medieval West* (SPCK, London 1965), pp. 101–108.

16. David Holeton, "The Communion of Infants and Young Children: A Sacrament of Community" in Geiko Müller-Fahrenholz (ed.), *And Do Not Hinder Them: An Ecumenical Plea for the Admission of Children to the Eucharist*, Faith and Order Paper no. 109 (World Council of Churches, Geneva 1982), p.

63. See also his *Infant Communion—Then and Now,* Grove Liturgical Study no. 27 (Grove Books, Bramcote Notts 1981).

17. DS, nos. 1730, 1734.

18. Canon 854.

19. See Eugene L. Brand, "Baptism and Communion of Infants: A Lutheran View," *Worship* 50 (1976), pp. 29–42.

20. For an excellent posing of the state of the question see Thomas F. Sullivan, "The Directory and First Confession," *The Living Light* 16 (1979), pp. 192–208. For a consideration of the 1983 Code of Canon Law's position on the obligation of first penance before first eucharist, see James H. Provost, "First Eucharist and First Penance," *The Jurist* 43 (1983), pp. 450–453.

21. An English translation can be found in Joseph B. Collins (ed.), *Catechetical Documents of Pope Pius X* (St. Anthony Guild Press, Paterson, N.J. 1946), pp. 54–62.

22. For example, Ladislas Orsy, *The Evolving Church and the Sacrament of Penance* (Dimension Books, Denville, N.J. 1978), p. 174: "Once such penitential services are offered to children, the widely disputed issue of what should come first, confession or communion, loses its importance."

23. *Sharing the Light of Faith: National Catechetical Directory for Catholics of the United States* (U.S. Catholic Conference, Washington, D.C. 1979), no. 126.

24. Aidan Kavanagh, "The Nature of Christian Penance,' pp. 11–12.

25. Collins, p. 59.

26. Ibid., pp. 60–61.

27. Ibid., pp. 59–60.

28. *Newsletter: Bishops' Committee on the Liturgy* 14 (1978), p. 110.

29. Ibid., p. 112.

30. Ibid., p. 111.

31. For a helpful treatment of the relationship between the

148

passages of the life cycle and the seven sacraments, see David Power, "The Odyssey of Man in Christ" in *Liturgy and Human Passage* (Seabury, New York 1979), pp. 100–111.

32. Daniel B. Stevick, "Christian Initiation: Post-Reformation to the Present Era" in *Made, Not Born* (University of Notre Dame Press, Notre Dame, Ind. 1976), p. 116.

33. Joseph F. Kett, *Rites of Passage: Adolescence in America 1790 to the Present* (Basic Books, New York 1977), pp. 5–6; 243.

34. *Sacrosanctum Concilium* 71, *Documents on the Liturgy* no. 71.

35. Bernard Botte, *Le Mouvement Liturgique: Témoignage et souvenirs* (Desclée, Paris 1973), p. 188.

36. See Schmemann, p. 79.

37. David M. Stanley, "The New Testament Doctrine of Baptism: An Essay in Biblical Theology," *Theological Studies* 18 (1957), pp. 207–208.

38. For a summary of the use of the words "confirmare" and "confirmatio" see J. D. C. Fisher, *Christian Initiation: Baptism in the Medieval West* (SPCK, London 1965), pp. 141–148.

39. See, for example, Seely Beggiani, "Christian Initiation in the Eastern Churches," *Living Light* 11 (1974), pp. 536–547.

40. Adrien Nocent, "Confirmation: the Difficult Catechesis," *Lumen Vitae* 28 (1973), p. 109.

41. Aidan Kavanagh, "Confirmation: A Suggestion from Structure," *Worship* 58 (1984), pp. 393–394. This article represents, as far as I can judge, a unique analysis of the question.

42. Ibid., p. 394, note 20.

43. Gabriele Winkler, "The Original Meaning of the Postbaptismal Anointing and Its Implications," *Worship* 52 (1978), p. 36.

44. Massey H. Shepherd, Jr., "Confirmation: The Early Church," *Worship* 46 (1972), p. 16.

45. *Summa Theologiae* III, q. 73, a. 3.

46. The 1983 Code of Canon Law states: "The sacraments of baptism, confirmation, and order, which imprint a character, cannot be repeated." Canon 845, 1.

47. J. Amougou-Atangana, *Ein Sakrament des Geistempfangs? Zum Verhältnis von Taufe und Firmung* (Freiburg-Basle-Vienna 1974), p. 301, as quoted by Günter Biemer, "Controversy on the Age of Confirmation as a Typical Example of Conflict between the Criteria of Theology and the Demands of Pastoral Theology," in David Power (ed.), *Liturgy and Human Passage* (Seabury, New York 1979), p. 115.

48. *Sacrosanctum Concilium* 71, *Documents on the Liturgy* no. 71.

49. Fisher, p. 139.

50. David Power, "The Odyssey of Man in Christ," *Liturgy and Human Passage* (Seabury, New York 1979), p. 101: "If there are then to be rituals for the key-moments of the life-cycle they have a form and a meaning distinct from the traditional sacraments."

Future of the Spirit

At this point in our inquiry frustration could well set in. It could be argued that present pastoral practice is so distanced from theological reality that the situation is hopeless. One might think, for example, that short of practicing infant confirmation, or at least confirmation before first eucharist, there is no way out of the dilemma.

While I certainly would like the present sacramental practice to change, I do not think that such a change would automatically solve our problems. What is needed is a change of attitudes. We must stop viewing initiation in a disjointed way and begin to see it as a unified process. Only with such a change of attitudes will a change in sacramental practice be made and indeed make sense. In the previous chapter, certain theological guidelines were set forth. Now, in the light of them and by way of conclusion, let me mention a few ways to effect such a reversal of attitudes.

The place to begin changing attitudes is with the sacrament of baptism. We have not made enough out of baptism. Even when we have paid attention to it, we have treated it too individualistically. The primary effect of the sacrament is a social one, making us members of Christ's Body. Modern preaching and teaching should emulate the third-century Syrian bishop who spurred his people on by the advice that they should not make light of their own baptized selves.[1] Christian teaching and preaching must be marked by the first of God's ecclesial gifts, baptism. If this is done, the gap between baptism and confirmation will begin to close. Confirmation will be viewed as belonging to baptism rather than as making up for the deficiencies of infant baptism. Antagonism will give way to complementarity. In this vein Catholics should also ask themselves what is being said when great fanfare is made over the confirmation of a baptized Christian coming into full communion with the Catholic Church. How does such fanfare redound on the previous baptism? Admittedly, the practice of anointing Christians coming into full communion does go back to the fourth century; nevertheless, we should ask ourselves if this is a good thing in our ecumenical age.

With such heightened awareness of baptismal consciousness, Christians will not reject infant baptism itself but only the indiscriminate baptism of infants. Likewise they will begin to push for change in the practices of the other initiation sacraments. The place to begin is on the parish and diocesan levels. Parents, religious educators, pastors, and bishops must dialogue in a context of study and charity. Once these groups realize that the best changes come from the grass roots, they should begin to ask such questions as: "Why cannot this four-year-old receive eucharist?" "Why cannot this baby be confirmed as well as baptized?" Answering such questions merely by referring to present liturgical law will not do justice to the dynamic sacramental life of the church.

This questioning will be enriched if it is done in an ecumenical framework. The Orthodox tradition of preserving the full initiation of infants and the communicating of children reflects pristine Christian practice. We must ask ourselves if the historical reasons for changing that practice in the West were sufficient, and if they justify any longer the dismemberment of the initiation

152

sacraments. Sections of this book dealt with Anglican and Protestant reforms precisely because these reforms have much to offer the Roman Catholic quest for solutions. The Anglican and Protestant rites make it clear that their "confirmation" is the mature reaffirmation of a previous baptism. That is not what Roman Catholics have understood confirmation to be in their own tradition. Yet gradually this perspective has gained ground among many Catholics. For them it is a rite of passage from adolescence into young Christian adulthood.

This shift of meaning of confirmation to a rite of passage dramatically underscores the need for rites of commitment at many stages in the Christian life, and not just at adolescence. The "Statement on Christian Commitment" of the Bishops' Committee on the Liturgy, discussed in chapter 6, has not yet received the attention it deserves. Liturgy committees as well as religious educators need to heed this important document, which offers multiple options for rites of commitment. The Christian life demands saying yes at each step of life's pilgrimage, not just at the time of entry into young Christian adulthood. Working with adolescents is necessary, but the church must be equally concerned with young adults as well as middle-aged and aging members.

Another attitude demanding reversal is revealed by parishes that give priestly stoles to the confirmation candidates, and by religious education materials that portray confirmation as a kind of lay ordination. Confirmation is part of the initiation process culminating in the eucharist, not a second-class ordination. The same error can be perpetrated by the use of oil and chrism. The fundamental and most significant use of these elements is in the ritual of Christian initiation where they symbolize the new Christians' sharing in the life of the anointed one, Jesus Christ. They, like Christ, are anointed with the Spirit. Catholics sometimes forget this point and view the priest as the only "anointed one." They forget the sacrament of order exists only to serve the sacraments of initiation. The priesthood of the ordained is not over and against, or outside of, the priesthood of all believers. It is part of it and stands in relation to it as the part serving the whole. Among those sharing in the priesthood of Christ through Christian initiation, some are ordained to ministries of special service. All, laity and clergy alike, are called to election and holiness. All are "a chosen race, a royal priesthood, a holy nation, God's own people" (1 Pt 2:9). An awareness of this fact gives meaning and dignity to the Christian life and to the liturgical uses of water, oil and chrism, bread and wine. It will, one hopes, bring an end to the harmful dichotomy that exists between laity and clergy, with the clergy enjoying a "superior rank." This in turn will cause a change in attitudes. Becoming a Christian will be what really counts. Confirmation as a kind of lay ordination will be seen to miss the mark.

A final reversal of attitudes will come from seeing the *entire* Christian life as a life in the Spirit. This life, begun in baptism and confirmation, is brought to completion in the eucharist. The eucharist is *the* sacrament of the Spirit. The eucharist is the way *par excellence* for Christians to reaffirm their baptism and confirmation, to become all the more that which they already are—the body of Christ. As Augustine says: "If then you are the body of Christ and his members, it is your sacrament that reposes on the altar of the Lord. It is your sacrament which you receive. You answer 'Amen' to what you yourself are. . . . Be what you see, and receive what you are."[2]

The chief opportunity, then, to reaffirm our baptism lies in the eucharist. At the eucharist we celebrate both the unity of the Body of Christ and pray for a healing of disunity in that Body, until the day when the Lord will come again to make all one. The eucharist is the repeatable sacrament of initiation. This repeatability calls for a change in attitudes. The eucharist is a means perfectly adapted to every stage and crisis of human existence. It is not something done once and for all at a key moment of the human life cycle; it is repeated time and again during the Christian life until life's final moment when an ultimate "yes" is uttered. Christian initiation finds its apex in the act of Christian death.

These concluding remarks are meant primarily as a plea to view confirmation in its proper context. Viewing the sacrament as a unique and isolated moment in the Christian life can create a letdown later on, or even worse, a failure to recognize continued gifts of the Spirit. The Christian life is one of mission to the world, and this involves frequent moments of commitment and even more frequent movements of the Spirit. This life begins with the sacraments of initiation—baptism, confirmation, eucharist. The Spirit cannot be separated from the Christian life. Why, then, separate the sacrament of confirmation, the gift of the Spirit, from the sacraments that celebrate initiation into the Christian life? Do we not give the impression that the Spirit is dormant until we take the initiative to commit ourselves? Do we not imply that the gift of the Spirit is not part of incorporation into the body of Christ?

Confirmation, and indeed the use of oil and chrism as well, must ever be viewed in the larger context—the Christian life as a life of the Spirit, a Pentecost life. The future of the church is that of the future of the Spirit, a Spirit urging all to become one in Christ to the glory of God the Father.

NOTES

1. *Didascalia Apostolorum,* Ch. 13. See R. H. Connolly (ed.), *Didascalia Apostolorum* (Clarendon Press, Oxford 1929), p. 124.

2. Augustine, *Sermo 272:* translation in André Hamman (ed.), *The Mass: Ancient Liturgies and Patristic Texts* (Alba House, Staten Island 1967), pp. 207–208.

Bibliography

The following titles all appear in the notes. Comments on the books or articles are sometimes added either in the notes or in this bibliography, which is divided into sections devoted to sources and to literature about the sources.

SOURCES

Acta Pontificae Commissionis Centralis Praeparationae Concilii Oecumenici Vaticani II 2. Typis Polyglottis Vaticanis, Vatican City 1962.

Aquinas, Thomas. *Summa Theologiae* III, qq. 60–65. In *The Sacraments*, Vol. 56, translated and edited by David Bourke. McGraw-Hill, New York 1975.

―――. *Summa Theologiae* III, qq. 66–72. In *Baptism and Confirmation*, vol. 57, translated and edited by James Cunningham with appendices by Gerard Austin. McGraw-Hill, New York 1975.

Augustine. *Sermo 272.* In *The Mass: Ancient Liturgies and Patristic Texts*, edited by André Hamman, pp. 206–208. Alba House, Staten Island 1967.

Baptism, Eucharist and Ministry. Faith and Order Paper 111. World Council of Churches, Geneva 1982. This is frequently referred to as the "Lima Text," being the product of a World Council meeting in Lima, Peru.

The Book of Common Prayer. Seabury, New York 1979.

Catechetical Documents of Pope Pius X, translated and edited by Joseph B. Collins. St. Anthony Guild Press, Paterson, N.J. 1946.

Codex Iuris Canonici. Typis Polyglottis Vaticanis, Vatican City 1918 and 1983. (English translation of the latter: *Code of Canon Law,* translation prepared under the auspices of the Canon Law Society of America, Washington, D.C. 1983).

Cyril of Jerusalem. *St. Cyril of Jerusalem's Lectures on the Christian Sacraments,* edited by F. L. Cross. SPCK, London 1960.

Didascalia Apostolorum, the Syriac version translated and accompanied by the Verona Latin fragments, with an introduction and notes by R. H. Connolly. Clarendon Press, Oxford 1929.

Documents on the Liturgy 1963–1979: Conciliar, Papal and Curial Texts. International Commission on English in the Liturgy, A Joint Commission of Catholic Bishops' Conferences. The Liturgical Press, Collegeville, Minn. 1982. This is a 1,500-page compilation of 554 official documents. An indispensable tool.

Enchiridion Symbolorum, 36th ed., edited by H. Denzinger and A. Schönmetzer. Herder, New York 1976.

Fisher, J. D. C. *Christian Initiation: The Reformation Period.* SPCK, London 1970. This supplies the rites of baptism and confirmation produced by the reformers together with other documents revealing the circumstances in which these rites were compiled and used. It covers the period from 1520 to 1552.

Gregory the Great. *Epistula XI.* In *Monumenta Germaniae Historica 2,* edited by Louis Hartmann. Weidmann, Berlin 1899.

Hippolytus. *La Tradition Apostolique de Saint Hippolyte,* edited by Bernard Botte. Aschendorf, Münster 1963.

————. *The Apostolic Tradition.* In Whitaker, *Documents of the Baptismal Liturgy,* pp. 2–7.

Holy Baptism: Together with a Form for Confirmation or the Laying-on of Hands by the Bishop with the Affirmation of Baptismal Vows, edited by Standing Liturgical Committee. Prayer Book Studies 26. Church Hymnal, New York 1973.

Irenaeus. *Contre les hérésies,* Livre III, edited by A. Rousseau and L. Doutreleau, Sources Chrétiennes 211. Editions du Cerf, Paris 1974.

Jagger, Peter J. *Christian Initiation: 1552–1969*. SPCK, London 1970. This work continues where the J. D. C. Fisher collection leaves off.

Leo the Great. *Ep. 159. Patrologia Latina* 54, cols. 1138–1139.

Lutheran Book of Worship. Augsburg, Minneapolis 1978.

Missale Gothicum, edited by L. C. Mohlberg. Herder, Rome 1961.

One Baptism, One Eucharist and a Mutually Recognized Ministry. Faith and Order Paper 73. World Council of Churches, Geneva 1975. This reflects the World Council's work of a period extending over fifty years.

Les Ordines Romani du Haut Moyen-Age III, edited by M. Andrieu. Spicilegium Sacrum Lovaniense, Louvain 1961.

Ordo Benedicendi Oleum Catechumenorum et Infirmorum et Conficiendi Chrisma. Typis Polyglottis Vaticanis, Vatican City 1971.

Ordo Confirmationis. Typis Polyglottis Vaticanis, Vatican City 1971.

Ordo Dedicationis Ecclesiae et Altaris. Typis Polyglottis Vaticanis, Vatican City 1977.

The Plan for Reunion, 3rd ed. Joint Committee on Presbyterian Union, New York 1981.

Le Pontifical Romain au Moyen-Age I: *Le Pontifical Romain du XIIe Siècle*, edited by M. Andrieu, Studi e Testi 86. Biblioteca Apostolica Vaticana, Vatican City 1938.

Le Pontifical Romain au Moyen-Age III: *Le Pontifical de Guillaume Durand*, edited by M. Andrieu, Studi e Testi 88. Biblioteca Apostolica Vaticana, Vatican City 1940.

Le Pontifical Romano-Germanique du dixième siècle, edited by C. Vogel and R. Elze, 2 vols. Studi e Testi 226, 227. Biblioteca Apostolica Vaticana, Vatican City 1963.

Rite of Baptism for Children. U.S. Catholic Conference, Washington, D.C. 1969.

Rite of Christian Initiation of Adults. U.S. Catholic Conference, Washington, D.C. 1974.

Rite of Confirmation. U.S. Catholic Conference, Washington, D.C. 1975.

The Rites of the Catholic Church. Pueblo, New York 1976. Among the rites contained here are Rite of Confirmation, Rite of the Blessing of Oils; Rite of Consecrating the Chrism.

The Rites of the Catholic Church II. Pueblo, New York 1980. Also contains Rite of the Blessing of Oils-Rite of Consecrating the Chrism.

Rituale Romanum. Sumptibus et Typis. Benziger Brothers, New York 1953.

The Roman Ritual, edited by Philip T. Weller. Bruce, Milwaukee 1964.

Le Sacramentaire Gélasien d'Angoulême, edited by P. Cagin. Edition diplomatique, Angoulême 1918.

Liber Sacramentorum Romanae Aeclesiae Ordinis Anni Circuli (Sacramentarium Gelasianum), edited by L. C. Mohlberg. Herder, Rome 1960.

A Service of Baptism, Confirmation and Renewal, revised edition. Supplemental Worship Resources 2, edited by Task Force on Baptism, Confirmation and Renewal. Parthenon Press, Nashville 1980. Contains the new rites of the United Methodist Church.

Sharing the Light of Faith: National Catechetical Directory for Catholics of the United States. U.S. Catholic Conference, Washington, D.C. 1979.

Tertullian. *On Baptism.* In *Tertullian's Homily on Baptism,* edited by Ernest Evans. SPCK, London 1964.

Vatican Council II: The Conciliar and Post Conciliar Documents, edited by A. Flannery. Costello, Northport, N.Y. 1981.

Whitaker, E. C., editor. *Documents of the Baptismal Liturgy,* 2nd ed. SPCK, London 1970. Second edition is revised and supplemented. Along with Fisher and Jagger it forms an indispensable English-language trilogy of chronologically ordered baptismal texts.

160

LITERATURE

Abbo, J. A. and J. D. Hannan. *The Sacred Canons*, 2 vols. Herder, St. Louis and London 1952.

Aland, Kurt. *Did the Early Church Baptize Infants?*, translated by G. R. Beasley-Murray. Westminster Press, Philadelphia 1963.

Austin, Gerard. "The Essential Rite of Confirmation and Liturgical Tradition." *Ephemerides Liturgicae* 86 (1972) 214–224.

———. "What Has Happened to Confirmation?" *Worship* 50 (1976) 420–426.

Balhoff, Michael James. Unpublished doctoral dissertation. "The Legal Interrelatedness of the Sacraments of Initiation: New Canonical Developments in the Latin Rite from Vatican II to the 1983 Code of Canon Law." The Catholic University of America 1984. A unique help in that the author uses documentation otherwise impossible to obtain.

Barth, Karl. *The Teaching of the Church Regarding Baptism*, translated by E. A. Payne. SCM Press, London 1948.

Beggiani, Seely. "Christian Initiation in the Eastern Churches." *Living Light* 11 (1974) 536–547.

Béraudy, Robert. "Initiation chrétienne." In *L'Eglise en Prière*, edited by A. G. Martimort, pp. 528–584. Desclée, Paris 1965.

Biemer, Günter. "Controversy on the Age of Confirmation as a Typical Example of a Conflict Between the Criteria of Theology and the Demands of Pastoral Theology." In *Liturgy and Human Passage*, edited by David Power, pp. 115–125. Seabury, New York 1979.

Botte, Bernard. "A propos de la confirmation." *Nouvelle Revue Théologique* 88 (1966) 848–852.

———. *Le Mouvement Liturgique: témoignage et souvenirs.* Desclée, Paris 1973. Insights by a key figure in the modern liturgical movement.

———. "Postbaptismal Anointing in the Ancient Patriarchate of Antioch." In *Studies on Syrian Baptismal Rites*, edited by Jacob Vellian, The Syrian Churches Series 6, pp. 63–71. CMS Press, Kottayam 1973.

Brand, Eugene L. "Baptism and Communion of Infants: A Lutheran View." *Worship* 50 (1976) 29–42.

Brown, Raymond. "The Challenge of the Three Biblical Priesthoods." *Catholic Mind* 78 (1980) 11–20.

————. "We Profess One Baptism for the Forgiveness of Sins." *Worship* 40 (1966) 260–271. An excellent summary of the practice of initiation in the New Testament period.

Calabuig, Ignazio M. *The Dedication of a Church and an Altar: A Theological Commentary.* U.S. Catholic Conference, Washington, D.C. 1980.

Chavasse, Antoine. *Le sacramentaire gélasien.* Desclée, Paris 1958.

Connor, James L. "Original Sin: Contemporary Approaches." *Theological Studies* 29 (1968) 215–240.

Cullmann, Oscar. *Baptism in the New Testament,* translated by J. K. S. Reid. SCM Press, London 1950.

Davenport, E. H. *The False Decretals.* Blackwell, Oxford 1916.

Daniélou, Jean. *The Bible and the Liturgy.* University of Notre Dame Press, Notre Dame, Ind. 1956.

Didier, J. C. *Faut-il baptiser les enfants? La réponse de la tradition.* Cerf, Paris 1967.

————. "Saint Augustin et le baptême des enfants." *Revue des Etudes Augustiniennes* 2 (1956) 109–129.

Diekmann, Godfrey. "The Laying on of Hands: The Basic Sacramental Rite." *Proceedings of the Catholic Theological Society of America* 29 (1974) 339–351.

Dillon, Richard J. and Joseph A. Fitzmyer. "Acts of the Apostles." In *The Jerome Biblical Commentary,* edited by Raymond Brown, Joseph Fitzmyer, and Roland Murphy, pp. 165–214. Prentice-Hall, Englewood Cliffs, N.J. 1968.

Dix, Gregory. *The Theology of Confirmation in Relation to Baptism.* Dacre Press, London 1946.

Dulles, Avery. "Toward a Christian Consensus: The Lima Meeting." *America* 146 (1982) 126–129.

162

Dunn, James D. G. *Baptism in the Holy Spirit.* SCM Press, London 1970.

────. "Spirit, Holy." In *The New International Dictionary of New Testament Theology* 3, edited by Colin Brown, pp. 693–707. Zondervan, Grand Rapids, Mich. 1975.

Finnegan, Eugene M. Unpublished doctoral dissertation. "The Origins of Confirmation in the Western Church: A Liturgical-dogmatic Study of the Development of the Separate Sacrament of Confirmation in the Western Church Prior to the Fourteenth Century." Theological Faculty of Trier, West Germany 1970. This extremely thorough study is available through the University of Notre Dame library.

Fisher, J. D. C. *Christian Initiation: Baptism in the Medieval West.* SPCK, London 1965. This work is indispensable for the study of the historical development of Christian initiation.

Flemington, W. F. *The New Testament Doctrine of Baptism.* SPCK, London 1964.

Fuller, Reginald. "Christian Initiation in the New Testament." In *Made, Not Born,* pp. 7–31. University of Notre Dame Press, Notre Dame, Ind. 1976.

Gallen, John. "American Liturgy: A Theological Locus." *Theological Studies* 35 (1974) 302–311.

Gasparri, P. *Codicis Iuris Canonici Fontes* III, IV. Typis Polyglottis Vaticanis, Vatican City 1925 and 1926.

Greenstock, David L. "The Problem of Confirmation." In *The Thomist Reader: Texts and Studies,* pp. 119–239. Thomist Press, Washington, D.C. 1957.

Gy, P. M. "Histoire liturgique du sacrement de confirmation." *La Maison-Dieu* 58 (1959) 135–145.

────. "Quamprimum. Note sur le baptême des enfants." *La Maison-Dieu* 32 (1952) 124–128.

Hatchett, Marion. *Commentary on the American Prayer Book.* Seabury, New York 1980. A companion to the American *Book of Common Prayer* of 1979.

────. "The Rite of 'Confirmation' in the Book of Common

Prayer and in Authorized Services 1973." *Anglican Theological Review* 56 (1974) 292–310.

Henderson, Frank J. "The Chrism Mass of Holy Thursday." *Worship* 51 (1977) 149–158.

Hofmeister, Philipp. *Die heiligen Öle in der morgen- und abendländischen Kirche.* Augustininus-Verlag, Würzburg 1948. A classic study.

Holeton, David R. "Christian Initiation in Some Anglican Provinces." *Studia Liturgica* 12 (1977) 129–150.

––––––. "The Communion of Infants and Young Children: A Sacrament of Community." In *And Do Not Hinder Them: An Ecumenical Plea for the Admission of Children to the Eucharist,* edited by Geiko Müller-Fahrenholz, Faith and Order Paper no. 109, pp. 59–69. World Council of Churches, Geneva 1982.

––––––. *Infant Communion—Then and Now.* Grove Liturgical Study no. 27. Grove Books, Bramcote Notts 1981.

Holland, Bernard G. *Baptism in Early Methodism.* Epworth Press, London 1970.

Holmes, Urban T. *Confirmation: The Celebration of Maturity in Christ.* Seabury, New York 1975.

Jasper, Ronald C. D. "Christian Initiation: The Anglican Position." *Studia Liturgica* 12 (1977) 116–125.

Jeremias, Joachim. *Infant Baptism in the First Four Centuries,* translated by D. Cairns. Westminster Press, Philadelphia 1962.

Jounel, Pierre. "La consécration du chrême et la bénédiction des saintes huiles." *La Maison-Dieu* 112 (1972) 70–83.

Kavanagh, Aidan. "Confirmation: A Suggestion from Structure." *Worship* 58 (1984) 386–395.

––––––. "The Nature of Christian Penance: Metanoia and Reconciliation." *Resonance* 2 (1966) 8–14.

––––––. *The Shape of Baptism: The Rite of Christian Initiation.* Studies in the Reformed Rites of the Catholic Church, vol. 1. Pueblo, New York 1978. A most valuable study.

164

Kett, Joseph F. *Rites of Passage: Adolescence in America 1790 to the Present.* Basic Books, New York 1977. An important work for the modern concept of adolescence.

Kretschmar, Georg. "Die Geschichte des Taufgottesdienstes in der alten Kirche." In *Leitourgia. Handbuch des evangelischen Gottesdienstes 5*, pp. 1–348. J. Stauda Verlag, Kassel 1970.

Lampe, G. W. H. *The Seal of the Spirit. A Study in the Doctrine of Baptism and Confirmation in the New Testament and the Fathers*, 2nd ed. SPCK, London 1967.

Lengeling, Emil. "Blessing of Baptismal Water in the Roman Rite." In *Adult Baptism and the Catechumenate*, edited by J. Wagner, *Concilium* 22, 62–68. Paulist Press, New York 1967.

Levesque, Joseph L. "The Theology of the Postbaptismal Rites in the Seventh and Eighth Century Gallican Church." *Ephemerides Liturgicae* 95 (1981) 3–43.

Ligier, Louis. *La confirmation: sens et conjoncture oecuménique hier et aujourd'hui.* Théologie Historique 23. Beauchesne, Paris 1973. This work synthesizes a wealth of material, especially the Eastern practices, and deserves singular attention.

————. "Le nouveau rituel du baptême des enfants." *La Maison-Dieu* 98 (1969) 7–31.

Llopart, Estanislau M. "Les Fórmules de la Confirmació en el Pontifical Romà." In *Liturgica* 2, Scripta et documenta 10, pp. 121–180. Tallers Gràfics Marià Galve, Barcelona 1958. A unique source for the various formulas that have been used for confirmation. Series by Abbey of Montserrat.

Macdonald, J. "Imposition of Hands in the Letters of Innocent I." In *Studia Patristica* II, 49–53. Akademie-Verlag, Berlin 1957.

Marsh, Thomas. "A Study of Confirmation." *Irish Theological Quarterly* 39 (1972) 149–163.

Martimort, A. G., editor. *L'Eglise en Prière.* Desclée, Paris 1965. A helpful manual of liturgical studies, part of which has been translated into English as *The Church at Prayer*, translated by R. Fisher *et al.* Irish University Press, New York 1968.

McDermott, Brian. "The Theology of Original Sin: Recent Developments." Theological Studies 38 (1977) 478–512.

Mitchell, Leonel L. Baptismal Anointing. SPCK, London 1966.

————. "The Theology of Christian Initiation and the Proposed Book of Common Prayer." Anglican Theological Review 60 (1978) 399–419.

————. "What is Confirmation?" Anglican Theological Review 55 (1973) 201–212.

Mongoven, Anne Marie. Signs of Catechesis. Paulist Press, New York 1979.

Morin, G. "Une particularité arlésienne de la liturgie du samedi saint." Ephemerides Liturgicae 49 (1935) 146–149.

Mouhana, Augustin. Les rites de l'initiation dans l'église Maronite. Orientalia Christiana Analecta 212. Pontificium Institutum Studiorum Orientalium, Rome 1978

Neunheuser, Burkhard. Baptism and Confirmation. Herder and Herder, New York 1964.

Nocent Adrien. "Confirmation: The Difficult Catechesis." Lumen Vitae 28 (1973) 97–109.

Orsy, Ladislas. The Evolving Church and the Sacrament of Penance. Dimension Books, Denville, N.J. 1978.

Pelikan, Jaroslav. The Christian Tradition 1: The Emergence of the Catholic Tradition (100–600). University of Chicago Press, Chicago 1971.

Pfatteicher, Philip H. and Carlos R. Messerli. Manual on the Liturgy: Lutheran Book of Worship. Augsburg, Minneapolis 1979.

Porter, Harry Boone. Jeremy Taylor, Liturgist. SPCK, London 1979.

de la Potterie, Ignace and Stanislaus Lyonnet. The Christian Lives by the Spirit, Alba House, Staten Island, N.Y. 1971. Very helpful for a theology of the Holy Spirit.

Power, David. "The Odyssey of Man in Christ." In Liturgy and Human Passage, edited by D. Power and L. Maldonado, pp. 100–111. Seabury, New York 1979.

Price, Charles P. and Louis Weil. *Liturgy for Living.* Seabury, New York 1979.

Provost, James H. "First Eucharist and First Penance." *The Jurist* 43 (1983) 450–453.

Quinn, Frank C. Unpublished doctoral dissertation. "Contemporary Liturgical Revision: The Revised Rites of Confirmation in the Roman Catholic Church and in the American Episcopal Church." University of Notre Dame 1978. Extremely helpful for both Roman and Anglican developments of confirmation.

Rasmussen, Niels. "The Chrism Mass: Tradition and Renewal." In *The Cathedral: A Reader,* pp. 29–33. U.S. Catholic Conference, Washington, D.C. 1979.

Repp, Arthur C. *Confirmation in the Lutheran Church.* Concordia, St. Louis 1964.

Riley, Hugh M. *Christian Initiation: A Comparative Study of the Interpretation of the Baptismal Liturgy in the Mystagogical Writings of Cyril of Jerusalem, John Chrysostom, Theodore of Mopsuestia and Ambrose of Milan.* Catholic University of America Press, Washington, D.C. 1974. A most helpful tool.

Rodriguez, Antonio Mostaza. "The Minister of Confirmation." In *The Sacraments in Theology and Canon Law,* edited by N. Edelby, T. Jiménez-Urresti, and P. Huizing, pp. 28–36. Paulist Press, New York 1968.

Rogues, Jean. "La Préface Consécratoire du Chrême." *La Maison-Dieu* 49 (1957) 35–49.

Schmemann, Alexander. *Of Water and the Spirit.* St. Vladimir's Seminary Press, Crestwood, N.Y. 1974.

Schnackenburg, Rudolf. *Baptism in the Thought of St. Paul.* Herder and Herder, New York 1964.

Seasoltz, Kevin R. *New Liturgy, New Laws.* Liturgical Press, Collegeville, Minn. 1980.

Segelberg, E. "The Benedictio Olei in the Apostolic Tradition of Hippolytus." *Oriens Christianus* 48 (1964) 268–281.

Shepherd, Massey H. "Confirmation: The Early Church." *Worship* 46 (1972) 15–21.

Stanley, David M. "The New Testament Doctrine of Baptism: An Essay in Biblical Theology." *Theological Studies* 18 (1957) 169–215.

Stevick, Daniel B.. "Christian Initiation: Post-Reformation to the Present Era." In *Made, Not Born,* pp. 99–117. University of Notre Dame Press, Notre Dame, Ind. 1976.

————. *Holy Baptism Together With a Form for the Affirmation of Baptismal Vows With the Laying-on of Hands by the Bishop Also Called Confirmation.* Supplement to Prayer Book Studies 26. Church Hymnal Corporation, New York 1973.

————. "The Liturgics of Confirmation." In *Confirmation Reexamined,* edited by Kendig B. Cully, pp. 61–79. Morehouse-Barlow, Wilton, Conn. 1982.

Stookey, Laurence H. *Baptism: Christ's Act in the Church.* Abingdon Press, Nashville 1982.

Sullivan, Thomas F. "The Directory and First Confession." *The Living Light* 16 (1979) 192–208.

Van Buchem, L. A. *L'Homélie Pseudo-Eusébienne de Pentecôte: l'origine de la confirmation en Gaule Méridionale et l'interprétation de ce rite par Fauste de Riez.* Drukkerij Gebr. Janssen N.V., Nijmegen 1967. An absolutely indispensable tool for the study of the history of confirmation.

Van den Eynde, Damien. "The Theory of the Composition of the Sacraments in Early Scholasticism." *Franciscan Studies* 12 (1952) 1–26.

Wainwright, Geoffrey. *Christian Initiation.* John Knox Press, Richmond 1969.

Weil, Louis. *Sacraments and Liturgy: The Outward Signs.* Blackwell, Oxford 1983.

Winkler, Gabriele. "Confirmation or Chrismation? A Study in Comparative Liturgy." *Worship* 58 (1984) 2–17.

————. *Das Armenische Initiationsrituale. Entwicklungsgeschichtliche und liturgievergleichende Untersuchung der Quellen des 3. bis 10. Jahrhunderts.* Orientalia Christiana Analecta 217.

Pontificium Institutum Studiorum Orientalium, Rome 1982. A monumental work for the study of the early church's baptismal theology.

―――. "Eine bemerkenswerte Stelle in armenischen Glaubensbekenntnis: Credimus et in Spiritum Sanctum qui descendit in Jordanem proclamavit missum." *Oriens Christianus* 63 (1979) 130–162.

―――. "The Original Meaning of the Prebaptismal Anointing and Its Implications." *Worship* 52 (1978) 24–45.

Wolf, Frederick B. "Christian Initiation." In *Prayer Book Renewal,* edited by J. Barry Evans, pp. 35–44. Seabury, New York 1978.

Ysebaert, J. *Greek Baptismal Terminology: Its Origins and Early Development.* Dekker and Van de Vegt N.V., Nijmegen 1962. Contains a very helpful section, "Imposition of Hands, Anointing, and Sealing," pp. 182–426.

Index

Fortitude, gift of, 19–20
Fuller, Reginald, 7, 31

Garment, baptismal, 24–25
Gelasianum Sacramentary, 66, 67, 103
Greenstock, David, 28, 37
Gregory the Great, pope, 16, 33

Hatchett, Marion, 66ff., 79, 81
Henderson, J. Frank, 113–114, 122
Heretics, reconciliation of, with Church, 15ff.
Hippolytus, 11, 100–101
Holeton, David, 130, 147
Holland, Bernard, 89f., 96
Holy Spirit, x, 4, 5, 6ff., 15, 16, 17, 19, 25–26, 43–44, 45, 46, 47, 48, 66, 70, 74, 76, 83, 85, 92, 97, 101, 109–110, 113, 118, 128–129, 137–139, 140, 141, 154, 155
Holy Thursday, 102f., 105, 112f.
Homily, 105, 112
Hugh of Saint Cher, theologian, 42
Hydatos, 5
Hylomorphism, 42–43

Imposition of hands, 15, 16, 22–23, 28–29, 43ff., 101. *See also* Laying on of hands
Infants, baptism of, 125–127
communion of, 129–130
complete initiation of, 128–131
Initiation, Christian, 3, 4f., 6ff., 9, 14, 17, 29, 41f., 47, 52, 54, 73, 83–84, 90, 113, 132, 135, 139, 140, 144, 155, 162
International Committee on English in the Liturgy (ICEL), 45–46
Irenaeus of Lyon, Saint, xi, xii, 15, 33
Isaiah, prophet, 3–4

Jesus, baptism of, 4ff.
John the Baptizer, xi, 3, 4ff.

Kavanagh, Aidan, xii, 5, 31, 41, 60, 132, 140, 146, 147, 148, 149
Kiss of peace, 20, 22
Kretschmar, G., 23–24